ENGLISH CHURCHES

Basil Clarke and John Betjeman

ENGLISH CHURCHES

LONDON HOUSE & MAXWELL
New York

Basil Clarke has been mainly responsible for the text, and John Betjeman for the choice of illustrations. In the selection and captioning of photographs, the authors have been ably assisted by Mr Rodney Hubbuck, who also contributed some of his photographs.

This book has been compiled with the particular collaboration of the National Buildings Record who have unstintingly made available their unique collection. All pictures, unless otherwise acknowledged on page 201, are reproduced by permission of the National Buildings Record. The authors would also particularly like to thank Mr John Piper, who permitted them to draw on the remarkable collection of his own photographs of churches.

© Basil Clarke 1964

First Published in The United States of America 1964 by
London House & Maxwell
A Division of the British Book Centre, Inc.
122 East 55th Street, New York 22, New York
Library of Congress Catalog Card No. 64-25398

First published 1964 by Studio Vista Ltd
Printed in Great Britain by W. & J. Mackay & Co Ltd Chatham Kent
Illustrated section printed by The Anchor Press Ltd Tiptree Essex

CONTENTS

TEXT

Romanesque   *page*   7

Early English and Decrated Gothic   15

Perpendicular Gothic   22

The Sixteenth and Seventeenth Centuries   31

The Eighteenth Century   35

The Nineteenth Century   40

The Twentieth Century   51

ILLUSTRATIONS

Preface to Pictures   55

Pre-Conquest   *illus.*   1–9

Post-Conquest   10–29

The Earlier Gothic   30–63

English Perpendicular   64–124

Early Post-Reformation   125–137

Medieval Churches adapted to Prayer Book Worship   138–147

Nonconformity   148–153

Stuart and Georgian   154–180

Memorials   181–188

Early Nineteenth Century   189–199

Victorian   200–210

Mid-Victorian Advance   211–228

Late Victorian and Edwardian   229–255

Modern   256–263

ACKNOWLEDGEMENTS   *page*   201

INDICES   203

ROMANESQUE

❀ ❀

CHURCHES BUILT BEFORE THE CONQUEST

The English Church was the result of missions from two directions: there were the Irish and Scottish missionaries in the north, and the missionaries from the Continent in the south.

In 664, at the Synod of Whitby, most of the Scots agreed to accept the customs of the rest of the Church in Europe, particularly in the matter of the calculation of the date of Easter. And in the next century the British Church in the west, which until then had gone its own way, was induced to do the same. There are no architectural remains of importance of the British Church; but some of the churches in remote parts of Wales, though much later in date, must give some idea of what a British church looked like.

The northern missionaries in the early days were not interested in building, and their churches were of wood. It is probable that many of them were not what we should call churches at all: there was simply a covering for the altar, and none for the congregation, who stood outside on the grass.

St Augustine was sent to Britain by Pope Gregory, and arrived in 597. He converted and baptized King Ethelbert of Kent, who gave him an old ruined church dating back to Roman days—the predecessor of Canterbury Cathedral. He also founded the monastery of SS Peter and Paul, of which the ruined church survives, and the church of St Pancras, part of which is still there. These, and the other churches built at this time, must have been the work of masons from abroad. Their style is crude provincial Romanesque, and their plan is probably derived from certain churches round about the Mediterranean. But there are not enough churches of this date, either here or there, to make it possible to say more exactly what the connexion is; and nothing is known about the builders of the English churches. They consist—or used to—of a nave with a semicircular apse, entered—in four cases, and perhaps originally in all—by three arches. There are projections at the sides (*porticus*) of which the purpose is doubtful. They may be the same as the *cubicula* of which St Paulinus of Nola writes, 'built for those who desired to pray or meditate on the word of God, and as memorials to the

7

departed'. St. Augustine himself, and five other bishops, were buried in the north porticus of SS Peter and Paul, and King Ethelbert and Queen Bertha in the south. At the west there is a porch. The use of this was originally for those who were preparing for baptism—the catechumens, who were neither in the Church nor out of it. But it is doubtful whether it could ever have been used for this in England: there were mass baptisms, for which there could have been little preparation; and infant baptism after that.

There are so few of these churches left that it is possible to mention particular examples.

Bradwell-on-Sea, Essex, was built by St Cedd after 653: the nave only remains. Reculver, Kent, was an interesting large church. In 669 the king granted the place to a priest called Bassa to build a monastery. The church had the usual Kentish plan; but about a hundred years later the porticus were extended to make chambers all down the sides of the nave. In 1805 most of the church was pulled down, but the outlines of the old work have been marked out on the grass.

Brixworth, Northamptonshire, is the finest of the surviving churches. A monastery was established here by 675, and there is no doubt that the church is of this date. It consisted of the present church, with aisles; at the west was a porch, and at the east an apse, entered by a triple arch. In 870 the church was burned by the Danes. Afterwards the aisles were taken down, and so were the north and south ends of the porch: the central portion of the porch was rebuilt as a tower.

The earliest surviving churches in the north are of about the same date as these—after the Synod of Whitby.

In 653 Benedict Biscop, a young Northumbrian, visited Rome with St Wilfrid. He went again in 665, and twice later, and came back with various books and relics, which so impressed the King of Northumbria that he gave him land on which to build a monastery, in honour of St Peter, in which to put his treasures. This was at Monkwearmouth, in the County of Durham. A year later, in 675, Benedict made a journey to Gaul to find masons to build the church. It was, we are told, 'built of stone after the Roman fashion, which the founder always loved'; and he had the windows glazed, and lamps and vessels made, by Frankish workmen. All the furniture and vestments, which Benedict could not get at home, he bought abroad. Later, he paid another visit to Rome, and procured John, the precentor of St Peter's, to teach his Northumbrian monks to sing the service. He also bought pictures to adorn the church.

The west end of Wearmouth remains, with a porch—far too small to hold catechumens—which was carried up as a tower, later, but still before the Norman Conquest.

Soon afterwards the king gave Benedict land at Jarrow to build a sister monastery of St Paul, and the church there was consecrated on April 23, 684 The chancel of Jarrow church is seventh-century: it is well built, of large blocks of stone, and has one or two original windows. The nave, which was rebuilt in the eighteenth century and again in the nineteenth, is on the site of the main church. The tower between the two was built in the eleventh century.

St Wilfrid built ambitious churches at Ripon and Hexham, but only the crypts remain.

Of about this time, or a little later, is the church of Escomb, County Durham, the real date of which was only discovered in the nineteenth century after it had been disused for a time. This is a complete church, and though it is partly built of Roman material, it is certainly not 'after the Roman fashion'. It has a tall and narrow nave, and a narrower square-ended chancel, separated by a simple round-headed arch.

It has been suggested that the rectangular chancel, which is, in effect, a separate chamber, is derived from the small cells that the northern missionaries built to protect the altar; and that this kind of church is, in fact, a compromise: a Celtic cell, tacked on to a nave to hold the congregation, such as the churches in the South had. This may be rather too simple a theory; but it is pleasant to be able to explain the typical parish church as a fusion of two elements, just as the English Church itself was.

The square east end became almost universal later on: the English never took kindly to the apse, which is rare at all times in England.

The years of the Danish invasions were not, of course, a time of church building, and the later pre-Conquest churches that exist mostly date from the tenth and eleventh centuries. The tenth century was a time of revival of monastic life, under St Dunstan, and some imposing churches were built, showing Carolingian influence. But all the larger churches, the cathedrals and abbeys have disappeared. What we have still are churches of the second rank, and complete churches are rare.

There are only three examples of aisled naves—Lydd, Kent (remains), Wing, Buckinghamshire, and Great Paxton, Huntingdonshire. The plan of most of the churches was an arrangement of rectangular chambers: nave, chancel, and porticus. There are some well-known towers of this time: the west end was the usual place, but in a few cases the base of the tower was the nave, with a porch to the west and a chancel to the east.

Walls are thin—in contrast to Norman walls, which are often very thick. The angles are either of large stones, or of long-and-short work: vertical and horizontal stones alternately. External walls are sometimes decorated with strips of stone.

Arches and doorways are not usually wide: the arches at Wing and at Worth

9

in Sussex are exceptional. They are almost always built of large stones, which go right through the wall, except at the very end of the period. Occasionally a doorway is triangular headed.

Windows are sometimes divided by a baluster in the centre, but usually they are small. A double splay—inside and out—is a sign of late pre-Conquest work.

Sculpture reached a high level in the North, but it was not much applied to buildings. Sculptured decorations seem to have been confined to one or two places: above the chancel arch, or over the entrance.

CHURCHES BUILT AFTER THE CONQUEST

The Norman Conquest brought the English Church into the main stream of European civilization, just at the beginning of one of the most eventful periods of the history of Christendom. England was part of Europe, and shared in its architectural development. Nevertheless, it had characteristics of its own, and it is possible to speak, as architectural writers did a hundred years ago, of an Anglo-Norman style.

When the occupation and pacification of the country were complete the Normans began a very large programme of church building and rebuilding. All the cathedrals and abbeys were rebuilt. The only bishop of English birth who was allowed to keep his position was Wulfstan of Worcester. He consented to a new cathedral being built, but he did not like it much. He said, 'We, poor wretches, destroy the works of our forefathers, only to get praise to ourselves. That happy age of holy men knew not how to build stately churches: under any roof they offered themselves as living temples to God. But we neglect the care of souls, and labour to heap up stones.'

Wulfstan was speaking rhetorically: all Saxon churches were not rude and contemptible, and in some ways the Saxons were finer artists than the Normans; but the new churches must certainly have seemed, by comparison, very ambitious. Several of the new cathedral and abbey churches had naves of an unprecedented length; and the Saxons had never attempted to build, as the Normans did, a stone church in every village.

The general appearance of a Norman church is well known. The walls are thick, but they are not as solid as they look: a Norman wall is often only a skin of masonry on both sides, filled in with rubble and mortar. Sometimes, in the more ambitious churches, there is an arcade on the interior face of the wall, which helps to hold it together. On the outside face the walls may be divided into bays by projecting pilasters. But the Normans were not very good at buttresses: they made the whole wall thick, instead of supporting it at certain places; and buttresses, where they exist, project very little.

There was an improvement in masonry about the middle of the century: early Norman work has wide joints, with a great deal of mortar; in the later work the joints are narrower. Herring-bone masonry used to be thought a sign of Saxon work: now, on the whole, it is considered more likely to be early Norman.

The plan of the ordinary smaller Norman church is nave and chancel: sometimes it is nave, chancel, and sanctuary, with or without a tower over the chancel. Some churches are cruciform. A west tower is not uncommon, but most towers have been added later. The east end is normally square. All the churches in Normandy itself have apses, and a few in England: but the English tradition of the square east end was very strong, and the apse never became popular. The square east end may be partly due to Cistercian influence: the Abbey of Waverley was founded in 1128.

There are plenty of Norman aisles, but they are not very common, in parish churches, in the earlier period. Some later Norman churches had aisles from the beginning, but many had them added after they were built: the stripping of plaster from the walls over the arcade has often revealed the remains of windows which are not much earlier than the arches which have been opened beneath them.

Arches are always semicircular. The Saxon builders liked large stones, and almost always built their arches of stones which go right through the wall. A Norman arch is made of small stones, sometimes with cut stones only at the edges: the middle of the arch, like the middle of the walls, was made of rubble.

Many arches are absolutely plain; but in doorways and chancel arches, and sometimes in nave arcades, the arch is often compound: one arch, with another, slightly larger, built on the top of it, and projecting slightly beyond it, and another on top of that—and so on. Each projection rests on shafts. This is not normally done on both sides of the wall. A doorway is compound only on the outside, and a chancel arch only on the west face: the inside of the doorway, and the east face of the chancel arch, are quite plain.

The arch of a doorway has often a stone filling, the tympanum, which is ornamented with carving: our Lord in glory, with the four evangelists; the Lamb of God, a cross, or the Tree of Life; and sometimes beasts, men fighting dragons, etc.

Ornament was, at the beginning, chopped out with an axe; later it was carved more sharply with a chisel, and sometimes quite deeply undercut. The most common is the zigzag or chevron, which is found almost everywhere. A variety of the zigzag is the beak-head. And there are many other ornaments which the nineteenth century listed and classified—the billet, lozenge, star, pellet, and so on —which occur in barbaric profusion on the more elaborate doorways and chancel arches.

Capitals are usually simple, though there is often figure carving on the capitals of smaller shafts. In early Norman days there is the cushion capital, a plain cube with the lower angles rounded off. The scalloped capital, which is sufficiently described by its name, is the most common type. There may be volutes at the corners, and sometimes, in the later work, there is simple foliage. The top member of the capital—the abacus—is square.

Stone vaults are not common in parish churches. Woodwork of any kind is now practically non-existent.

Fonts are the only piece of furniture of which a large number survives. Early Norman fonts are tub-shaped: the later ones are square, with a large central shaft and four smaller ones at the corners.

Almost every ancient church in the country is of Norman origin, if it is not earlier; and there may be Norman work somewhere in the church, even if it is not visible. Obviously, if a church has been enlarged in all directions since it was first built, there will not be much that can be seen. But often the wall above the nave arcades can be assumed to be Norman; and the wall on each side of the chancel arch, which would remain undisturbed through all the enlargements. (The same, of course, applies to the wall at the west end, on each side of the tower arch, unless the west end has been taken down and extended.)

The feature that has been most often saved is the doorway. If a church has been enlarged with an aisle, let us say on the south but not on the north, the lower part of the north wall is probably still Norman, even though the wall has been heightened and new windows have been inserted in it. A doorway often remains here, though it has usually been blocked. The more elaborate doorway on the south has been taken out, and rebuilt in the newer wall. It is not safe to assume that because the doorway is Norman the wall is Norman also.

The font was, as we have said, also spared in a great many churches. Sometimes it was recut with later ornament: if there is a font with later detail, but a Norman shape, it is safe to assume that it is really Norman in origin.

THE BEGINNINGS OF GOTHIC

By about 1160 the pointed arch is beginning to make its appearance. There were probably two main reasons for this.

(1) The pointed arch is stronger. A semicircular arch looks strong enough; but its weak point is at the top, where it is apt to give way. A pointed arch is called, in French, a broken arch, and that is what it is: two parts of an arch leant up against each other and supporting each other. And, provided the abutments are secure, the arch keeps itself up.

(2) The other reason is connected with the development of the stone-ribbed

vault. If you are vaulting a square space with semicircular arches, they will rise to different heights, as the diagonals of a square are longer than the sides of it. There are ways of getting round this; but the only satisfactory way is to make the arches pointed. A pointed arch can be made to rise to any height.

The ribbed vaulting at Durham Cathedral, with pointed arches, had been built as early as the beginning of the century. It did not lead to much else for the time being, though a few churches, such as Fountains Abbey, were given pointed barrel vaults in the aisles. But it must have opened out new possibilities. (This would not, it is true, affect the small churches, which, in England, hardly ever have a stone vault. But obviously it was not in the small churches that such things began. The constructional problems were worked out in the big churches, and the fashions spread to the smaller ones afterwards.)

Note. The word Gothic was used from the early seventeenth century onwards to describe buildings with pointed arches. It was, of course, a term of abuse, meaning barbarous; but by the nineteenth century it had become respectable, and it is still in general use.

Until the latter part of the eighteenth century no one had studied the subject carefully enough to know when Gothic began, how it began, or how it developed, and all kinds of wild guesses were made. But by the end of the century there were a few who took the trouble to investigate the matter carefully, and to acquire some understanding of the nature and history of English architecture. It began to be realized that the semicircular arch had been used before the Norman Conquest, and for about a hundred years after it; that the pointed arch had begun to come into use in the second half of the twelfth century; and that the pointed style had developed and blossomed out in the next three hundred years.

Thomas Rickman (1776–1841) co-ordinated what had been done, popularized the subject, and invented names for the various styles that are still in use today. His *Attempt to Discriminate the Styles of English Architecture* (1819) went through many editions and was revised by himself and others.

Rickman did not like the name Gothic much; but he kept it, and divided Gothic into three periods, corresponding roughly with the thirteenth, fourteenth, and fifteenth centuries—which he calls Early English, Decorated, and Perpendicular. He clearly distinguishes the characteristics of the styles, and gives a list of buildings of which the dates are known.

Later writers emphasized many things that Rickman had not dealt with—in particular the religious background and inspiration of medieval art, and the connexion between the buildings and the worship that went on (and still goes on) inside them. They also made it clear that English architecture did not stand all alone, but that it had to be studied in relation to that of the rest of Europe.

In this century there has been a new interest in the actual process of building and in the craftsmen who were engaged in it.

There is no end to the study of churches, and new discoveries are constantly being made. But Rickman's general outline remains unquestioned.

TRANSITIONAL

As Rickman saw, Gothic did not appear ready made: there is what he called the period of Transition (Trans. for short), when Norman features, and the features of the coming First Pointed style, were used together: sometimes more of the one, and sometimes more of the other. There may be an arch or a doorway which is pointed, but which has Norman ornaments; or there may, especially in some counties, be round-headed arches which have the ornaments of the coming style.

Transitional work is very unevenly distributed: there is a good deal in Northamptonshire, and there are some good examples on the upper Thames. In Kent it lasted on for some time, whereas in some other counties there is not much.

During the time of the Transition there was a development of carving. The capitals may be of the old scalloped shape, but they are more carefully done, and are beginning to show varieties. Foliage appears on capitals, and bases are more carefully carved. There may be deeply cut mouldings round the arch. The abacus is still normally square, though it may be octagonal. There is little or no crude, grotesque carving.

By about 1200, more or less, the new style was complete. Rickman gave the first phase of Gothic the name Early English. This is not very accurate: Gothic was making its appearance in France at the same time. But there are certainly some special features about English work, and the name is not likely to disappear.

EARLY ENGLISH AND DECORATED GOTHIC

✳ ✳

THE THIRTEENTH CENTURY

Early English (or First Pointed, as the more particular Victorians preferred to call it) lasted from about 1200 to 1260. After that, there was another period of Transition.

Churches of this date are found in some counties more than in others. Norfolk and Suffolk have almost none: there was so much rebuilding 200 years later that most of the earlier work has disappeared. In Sussex, on the other hand, practically every old church has work dating from the thirteenth century—most of it very simple and humble. Lincolnshire has fine work of every period, including much excellent Early English.

The characteristics of the style are easy to recognize and to remember.

Arches are now pointed. There are hang-over semicircular arches in some districts, but not many. The Early English window has been given the name of Lancet; and occasionally the whole style is called the Lancet style. Windows are seldom wide, and in the North they are very narrow. A rough test of date is whether the lancets are single or grouped. In the early part of the century they are usually single. There may be two, or three, in an east wall; but they are treated as separate windows, not set close together and contained under a single arch. Later on they begin to move together, and form a double or triple window, occasionally a group of five, and, once or twice, of seven.

Arches are usually compound, though often very simple, with the edge of each ring cut off at an angle of 45 degrees (a chamfer). In the more ambitious churches they have deeply cut mouldings.

Pillars are usually circular, but octagonal pillars are beginning to come in: they often alternate with circular ones in a nave arcade. The abacus has ceased to be square, and is, according to the shape of the pillar, circular or octagonal. In France the square abacus lasted right into the thirteenth century.

Capitals are moulded, or carved with foliage—which is always stiff-leafed. It does not represent any particular plant, though some of the Victorians tried to prove that it did. Sir Gilbert Scott once dreamed that he had found it, and awoke (or so he said), crying, 'Eureka, Eureka!' But it was only a dream, after all. Heads may appear among the foliage.

Bases are usually 'water-holding'. In some of the more elaborate churches the pillars are compound, sometimes with rings round the middle.

There is not much ornament. One is very characteristic: what is rather oddly called the dogtooth, which is, in fact, a pyramid cut into a kind of fourfold pointed leaf. Another is the nail-head, which is sometimes found in a ring round the capitals.

There are more Early English than Norman roofs surviving: they are always simple and high pitched.

Buttresses begin to project a great deal more, and to be constructed with set-offs: there are sometimes small gables on the top. At the corners there are generally two buttresses, not one set at an angle.

Porches are more common than in Norman times, and so are towers, though many churches, even quite large ones, have their bells hung in stone bell-cotes. Spires begin to appear in some districts.

While there are many complete Early English churches, there are far more that were simply enlarged during the period. This is not surprising, considering the enormous number of churches that had been built in the previous century. It was unnecessary to take down your Norman church; but you would be eager to improve it by building a longer chancel, or by adding aisles.

Early English aisles are nearly always lean-to, which makes the walls very low, and the lancets in them very small. Very many Early English aisles have been rebuilt and widened at a later date. But many have simply been raised and given larger windows. A later-looking aisle which is only a few feet wide can be assumed to keep its thirteenth-century width. The original height of the wall can often be seen at the east or the west end, with masonry added above its original roof-level to bring it to its present height.

Longer chancels were coming into fashion, and many Norman chancels have been rebuilt or extended.

Norman churches occasionally had a clearstory (an upper range of windows above the arcade). A clearstory is slightly more common in the thirteenth century. Sometimes the windows are circular, in the form of a quatrefoil. The projections which form the quatrefoil, or an open trefoil at the top of a lancet, are called cusps: cusped lancets are a sign of rather late Early English work.

Underneath the windows, or dividing a tower into stages, there may be a string course—a small projecting band of masonry which looks as though it has been tied round the building to hold it together. It may also go round higher up, at the level of the springing of the arches of the windows, and be looped up over the tops of them. Or there may be a small projecting moulding over the head of the arch, called a dripstone when it is outside, because its purpose is to throw off the rain, and a hood-mould when it is inside—with a small head, or a knot of foliage, or a mask-corbel, at the ends of it.

The nineteenth-century writers considered that Early English was imperfect, undeveloped Gothic. It is very easy to imitate, and many churches were built in Early English style in the 1840s. But it was felt that it was a little too easy, and that there was something lacking in it. It is true that Early English work can be rather dull; nevertheless there is a reticence and good taste and religious feeling about it, at its best, that are very obvious. There is no longer the barbarous and rather childish Norman ornament which was often spread about all over the place. Ornament is kept under control, and it is very well carved. And the religious influence is far stronger. This was the time when the religious orders were at the height of their prosperity and influence. And it was a time of considerable achievement in religious thought. Altogether, there is a far more free and happier feeling than there is in Norman work.

But it was only a beginning, and there was more to follow.

The first development was in the windows. The lancet may be a very beautiful form of window, but it has its limitations, and it may be rather dull. And many Early English churches must have been very dark, especially when there were lean-to aisles and no clearstory. Before the middle of the thirteenth century the designers were beginning to experiment by grouping lancets together, bringing them under one arch, and giving the arch internal shafts. And if two or three lancets are brought together and enclosed in that way, the obvious thing to do next will be to do something about the space above their heads. It can be pierced with a lozenge or with circles. And when that has been done it is only a step to treating it all as one window. The spaces between will cease to be pieces of wall and will be lightened to form stone bars. It will have become a single window divided by tracery. (It is not certain who invented that word. Sir Christopher Wren uses it, and it may be his: anyhow, it means the ramifications of the stone in the head of the window. The stone uprights are the mullions.)

The earliest tracery, when the parts of the window are still separated by pieces of wall, is called Plate Tracery, and the later development, when everything forms one window, is called Bar Tracery.

The earliest Bar Tracery is called Geometrical, for obvious reasons: it can all be easily drawn with a ruler and a pair of compasses. The head of the window is filled with circles, or segments of circles, or sometimes with a continuation of the lower lights, intersecting each other.

This can be thought of either as the latest development of Early English or as the beginning of the next style. The nineteenth-century writers usually treated it as the beginning of the next. But in fact it belongs more nearly to Early English: there is not much difference in the other features—the arches and the capitals.

To many of the Victorians this seemed the time when Gothic was at its best. It was still chaste, vigorous, and beautiful, but it had shaken off the immaturity of the earlier thirteenth-century work. The more modern writers see Gothic as developing all the time during the next two centuries. The builders learned more about construction, and were able to build more economically and scientifically.

There are not many complete churches of this period, but there are many that have had windows inserted or some alterations made. One result of the nineteenth-century admiration for this phase of Gothic was that a great deal of restoration work was done in this style; and there may well be more windows with Geometrical tracery that were made in the nineteenth century than there are thirteenth-century ones. Such windows need to be looked at carefully, especially if they are at the east end. Very many of them are nineteenth-century. They are not, of course, any the worse for that; but they cannot be taken as evidence that there was, in fact, work of the late thirteenth century in that particular church.

THE FOURTEENTH CENTURY

The name which Rickman gave to the next style was Decorated—which is not very helpful, as it is often quite plain. Others called it simply Middle, or Second Pointed. Others called it Curvilinear, which is an ugly word, but a far more descriptive title.

In the early part of the fourteenth century lines begin to curve. Geometrical tracery consists of circles and segments of circles, and the tops of the lights are two-centred. But now the ogee begins to appear, with its upward curve in the middle; and the lights of windows and the heads of tomb recesses, and sometimes of doorways, begin to be ogee-shaped. Larger doorways are usually of the ordinary shape, but the hood mould above may be an ogee.

The tracery of the windows breaks loose: the stone begins to bend, and it wanders in patterns about the head of the window. The nineteenth-century writers tried to classify Decorated tracery: and there is no harm in that, though there must be many subdivisions and overlappings, however it is done. There is no need to give many of the names that they used, but three of the more useful names are Reticulated (net-shaped), Leaf Tracery, and Flamboyant (flame-like—there is not much of this in England, but practically all French tracery is Flamboyant).

There are many very beautiful Decorated windows; and some that are less satisfactory and a little too ingenious. The obvious criticism of Decorated win-

18

dows, which has often been made, is that all the attention is concentrated on the lines of the stone, rather than on the shapes that they enclose. There are always left-over bits: there are certain to be, if a pattern is put inside a normal-shaped arch. It may be most satisfactory as a pattern, but it will produce some very odd shapes to be filled in by the glass-painter. Angels have to be fitted in at awkward angles, and there are small openings in which there is room for nothing but a piece of colour.

It is curious that at this time no one seems to have taken much trouble about doorways. They are usually quite plain, for it was windows that interested the designers.

Pillars are no longer circular: they are usually octagonal, and sometimes the capital is omitted. When they are compound the shafts are not as clearly distinguished as they were in the century before: they seem to have grown into one another.

Mouldings are not so deeply cut. The water-holding base has disappeared. The wave moulding is common.

When there is foliage it is no longer conventional and stiff-leafed: it is naturalistic—a copy of real leaves or flowers—and it is stuck on, or wrapped round, rather than growing from the capital itself. Crockets are naturalistic and creep in waves up the pinnacle or hood mould. The ball flower, a kind of circular, opening bud, takes the place of the dogtooth. Altogether there is a falling off in carved work: some of the carving is clever and pretty, but some is ugly and overdone. It was obviously meant to have a great deal of bright colour.

In the matter of plan, there is little change. Chancels continued to be large. Aisles began to be wider than they had been in the thirteenth century, and more chapels were added at the sides of chancels and elsewhere.

It should be made clear that the enlargement of churches was not done to provide accommodation for congregations. William Cobbett, who made his Rural Rides round England early in the nineteenth century, was constantly saying that the population had declined; and, to prove it, he pointed out the size of the old churches. They would now, he said, hold far more than the present population: therefore at the time when they were built there were far more people in the villages. But that is not a safe argument. The population was very small indeed compared with what it is now, but that did not mean that people did not enlarge their churches. They did not say, 'We must find room for so many people, and make our church the size that we need, and no larger.' There are large churches in places where the population has always been small.

They built partly because they liked it and wanted to. You can say, if you wish, that it was for the glory of God; and no doubt that was partly true. But there was often rivalry between parish and parish: if one improved its church, others would want to do the same.

The enlargements were also caused by the multiplication of altars. The number of priests was very large in proportion to the population, and each priest must say Mass daily. The earlier idea of the one Eucharist on Sunday, with a general Communion, had been superseded by the idea of as many Masses as possible—though the laity hardly ever communicated, except at Easter. We think of a church as a large place in which we can worship in common. The idea in the fourteenth and fifteenth centuries was of a kind of hall—the nave—surrounded by a number of separate chambers, screened off, and each with its own altar.

Many chantries were founded in the fourteenth century, and still more in the fifteenth; and the trade guilds maintained their chaplains and their altars, and often made benefactions for adorning the church or for adding to it.

There is this to be said, too: that the nave was not only used for worship. The chancel was, but the nave was often used as a kind of town hall and parish hall combined. Courts might be held there, and plays acted; and there might be dancing, and church ales. Things were certainly stored there, and markets might be held. The more spiritually minded churchmen did not approve of some of the things that went on in church, and tried to get them banished at least to the church-yard. But they were not very successful, and such things went on after the Reformation. One of the Homilies says that the church is the house of prayer, not the house of talking, of walking, of brawling, of minstrelsy, of hawks and dogs. It is well known that the nave of old St Paul's was used as a market-place and a place of meeting. But that was not exceptional: all kinds of things went on in church that we should not dream of allowing today.

In the fourteenth century fixed seats were beginning to come in, and they would obviously make a good deal of this more difficult. But even so, in some of the large churches in East Anglia there is, to this day, an empty space at the west of the nave—sometimes marked off by an additional screen, as at Walpole St Peter, and formerly at Boston. It is clear that other things besides worship went on there. The church was the centre of the common life of the parish.

The cruciform plan, with a central tower, fell out of favour. There are a few complete cruciform churches, with a tower over the crossing; but it is near enough to the truth to say that cruciform plans, in this century and in the next, are usually due to the reconstruction or rebuilding of older churches that were already of that shape.

Towers were becoming more prominent, and spires (in some parts of the country) were developing. Sometimes a central tower was taken down and a new one built at the west end.

The Black Death, in 1348–9, stopped building for a time. The Decorated style is supposed by some to have ended at this point; but it did not stop as abruptly as that. We may, if we wish to be neat and tidy, end it at 1360, as we ended the previous styles in the 60s of the twelfth and thirteenth centuries. But it went on after that. In Norfolk there was little change after the Black Death. But it is true that there was a sudden check, and that there was less of a Transitional period than there had been after the previous styles.

PERPENDICULAR GOTHIC

The new style was called Perpendicular by Rickman, and by others Rectilinear (the opposite of Curvilinear), meaning that the lines of windows were often carried up straight to the top of the arch instead of being curved.

The beginnings of the style are now usually connected with the school of designers in London, under the influence of the Court, who built, for example, the Royal Chapel at Westminster and the Chapter House at Old St Paul's, and who worked at Windsor and Canterbury. But the earliest and most complete example of developed Perpendicular is the Abbey Church of Gloucester, now the Cathedral. Edward II, who was buried there, was regarded as a saint, and the Abbey became a place of pilgrimage. The offerings were enormous, and the monks could have rebuilt the whole of their church if they had wanted. But instead they remodelled the transepts and the choir: the south transept was begun in 1331, and the choir in 1351. The Norman arcade and triforium were kept, but all projecting mouldings were shaved off, and the whole thing was covered with a kind of stone grille. The clearstory was taken down and rebuilt with large windows filled with simple tracery and strong vertical lines. The roof was ceiled with a rich stone vault, supported on shafts which go from floor to capitals without a break. The entire east end was pulled down and filled with a window that is certainly Perpendicular.

The designer must have been a man of exceptional ability. But, whoever he was, Gloucester is not now allowed to claim him, and he cannot be given the credit for entire originality. The basic ideas of Perpendicular had been developed gradually by the masons working for the Court.

The Black Death killed many masons, and the new ones had to be trained and set to work as soon as possible, like teachers after a war. The new fashion was simpler and cheaper than the old, and it had won the day long before the end of the century.

It is possible, too, that the Black Death had sobered people down, and that they had lost their taste for the light-hearted Decorated style. Anyhow, the new style soon ousted the old. There are buildings that can be called Transitional with features of both. There are some windows that have flowing tracery which is stiffening into Perpendicular. (For some reason, windows with flowing tracery are often found in the top stages of towers that are certainly of fifteenth-century date.) The builders of some late fourteenth-century churches seem to have been rather hesitant in adopting the new fashions. But there are also many churches in which the Perpendicular style appears all complete.

THE FIFTEENTH CENTURY

The last phase of English Gothic lasted the longest. We may take about 1360 as its beginning, but it would be hard to find a date for its ending, and it might be said that it never did end.

It was the time when English architecture was at its most English. The Court builders may have borrowed some of their ideas from France in the first place, but there is nothing like developed Perpendicular in any other country.

It is also the commonest style. There are very few churches without something of this period; and those that now have none often lost what they had in restorations in the nineteenth century.

It was also the most democratic of the church-building periods. Money was now more spread out, and much of it was in the hands of the rich merchants, especially in the wool-producing areas.

The monasteries were in decline, and a number of them had been suppressed before the reign of Henry VIII. A wealthy person who wanted to build something would now certainly build, or rebuild, a parish church, not a monastery.

In some counties—Norfolk and Suffolk in the east, and Devon and Cornwall in the west—the great majority of churches was rebuilt. So it is not easy to describe a Perpendicular church: there are so many churches and they differ so much in different parts of the country. What have they in common?

Walls are reduced and windows increased. It had long been understood—since the fashion for large windows began in the later thirteenth century—that a wall does not need to be enormously thick, and that it does not need supporting all along: buttresses need be placed only where the thrust of the roof comes. Many large fifteenth-century churches are almost nothing but windows with buttresses between.

Windows are difficult to describe, as there are so many varieties. It is only partly true to say that mullions are carried up to the head—which was the idea in the mind of Rickman when he invented the term Perpendicular. But it is true to say that the lights of the tracery usually balance the main lights: usually two above to one below. And they are usually straight-sided—which, of course, gives a clear run to the glass-painter: there are large figures below, and a row of little ones above. Larger windows may be divided across the middle of the main lights by a horizontal bar—a transom.

In many windows the arch is of the usual shape, but it is often four-centred. Sometimes the arch is segmental, and sometimes the head of the window is flat (though this is not necessarily a Perpendicular feature: some fourteenth-century windows are square-headed, especially in certain counties).

It is at this time that the battlement comes into extensive use.

Doorways are usually four-centred, in a rectangular label.

Porches are usual, and often very much developed. The porch was used for various purposes: bargains and contracts were confirmed there, and the first part of the marriage service was held there. It was also the place where the priest met the godparents and the child at a baptism, and the first part happened at the door.

Historically, the porch began as the place for the catechumens, who were preparing for baptism, and its invariable place was at the west. But we have seen how, later on, when there was no catechumenate, it shrank to quite a small size. Then, later still, as at Monkwearmouth, it was sometimes carried up into a tower. In England the west became the usual place for the tower, and it became the cuckoo in the nest: the porch was pushed out and had to go round to the side. (West porches do exist, but they are not at all common.) Still, a tiny relic of their original use lingered on, in this first part of baptism, in which the child was, in theory, being enrolled as a catechumen. This remained in the first English Prayer Book of 1549, but it was left out in the second book, and since then the whole service has been at the font.

Porches in large churches often have upper chambers, which were used for various purposes. Things were stored there; sometimes they were used for sleeping in—perhaps by a priest who was to say Mass early the next morning; and probably in the fifteenth century—certainly later—they were used for teaching children.

This was certainly the great age of towers: none of the earlier towers compare with those of the fifteenth century.

The plan is straightforward: nave and chancel, with or without aisles. There was a tendency in the later churches to extend the chancel aisles—which, were of course, always chapels—the whole length of the chancel, or very nearly, so that there was only a small sanctuary projecting: with the result that the plan of the church became almost a complete rectangle. But inside, the chapels had their own screens, and the interior was much divided up.

Pillars are either octagonal or compound; often lozenge-shaped, with shafts.

Foliage is almost non-existent, except in Devonshire, but there is sometimes a conventional square flower.

Clearstories are much larger, and often flood the church with light. Perpendicular clearstories were added to many churches that were not otherwise rebuilt.

And this is the time of the finest roofs. Sometimes they are flat, or nearly so, and panelled. In some districts there are tiebeams and kingposts. Often they are arch-braced. In East Anglia there are the finest hammer-beam roofs. It must be remembered that these roofs, like the rest of the woodwork, were originally coloured. The fifteenth-century church builders would not have understood our liking for uncoloured oak.

LOCAL VARIETIES

There are obvious local types of churches in different parts of England. In general, the size and appearance of a church depended on the quality and type of stone available. But there are similarities of design which have nothing much to do with the materials used. Some important centres, where there was a great deal of building, would attract a large number of workmen, who would also be employed in the neighbourhood. And one striking work would often be reproduced somewhere else: if the parishioners had seen something that they admired, they would agree to have it copied. There was also a good deal of stonework executed at the quarries, and sent away ready made.

But it is often not possible to say why one design was so much approved of by the people in one district that it was reproduced again and again. There seems to be no particular reason: but so it was.

In *Devon* and *Cornwall* there are never clearstories. Nave and chancel are usually of the same height, and the chapels reach almost to the end of the chancel. Roofs are of the wagon or barrel type, and there are many screens. Arcades and windows are almost always of a standard pattern; and indeed in these counties it is not easy to remember the difference between one church and another. Towers are plain, sturdy, and impressive.

Somerset has many magnificent towers. For some reason, the bodies of the churches are rather inferior, the arcades in particular being ordinary.

Gloucestershire has some of the best of the large fifteenth-century churches.

The larger churches of *Wiltshire* are of much the same type, but they are sometimes rather coarse in their details: there are too many, and too large, grotesques.

The Perpendicular work of *Dorset* is very minor, but not undistinguished. There is a local fashion of using alternate bands of flint and stone.

Sussex has a few characteristic towers.

There is nothing much to be said about *Hampshire*, *Surrey*, and *Berkshire*.

Kent has some sensible-looking towers.

Bedfordshire has a local fashion of double belfry windows, and *Hertfordshire* has thin lead spires.

Huntingdonshire and *Northamptonshire* are parts of the country with better building stone. Towers and spires may be admirable.

Some of the churches of *Lincolnshire* are deservedly famous. The steeple of Louth is surely the finest in the country.

The finest of all fifteenth-century churches are in Norfolk and Suffolk. Here they are restrained in their outline, because stone was scarce and not to be wasted. A peculiar feature of East Anglia is flushwork: patterns made of thin slices of stone set in flint. The towers have none of the exuberance of those in Somerset: they are plainly battlemented, with small pinnacles at the angles only. A local peculiarity is to have small figures of saints instead of pinnacles. The roofs have been mentioned. Screen work is more distinguished than in the West, and better painted.

Midland Perpendicular tends to be rather ordinary.

In *Cheshire* and *Lancashire* there are some good specimens of very late work.

About such a large county as *Yorkshire* it is not easy to generalize. There are some fine towers; but generally towers tend to be rather low, with battlements and small pinnacles. The churches are also low, without high-pitched roofs.

There are a few fine fifteenth-century churches on the English side of Wales, which are over the border, but are certainly English work.

THE BUILDING AND FURNISHING OF A MEDIEVAL CHURCH

How were these churches built? In the nineteenth century there were two legends about them.

One was that they were built by monks, and that they were designed by monks, priests, and bishops. This belief was widely held by the early ecclesiologists, and had an interesting result. Some of the clergy said, 'It was done by clergy in the Middle Ages: why should it not be done by us?' The Rev. W. Gray wrote, 'Let me strongly advise the junior members of our University to qualify themselves for Holy Orders by a practical knowledge of architecture. It is no disgrace to follow such men as William of Wykeham.' Gray was himself diocesan architect for Newfoundland, and when he returned to England he designed one or two churches. Those clergy who went out as missionaries naturally had the most scope: but there were not a few parish priests in England who made designs for the rebuilding or restoration of their own churches. They proved that it was quite possible for clergy to plan churches, and even to help build them. But it did not follow that their reading of history was correct, and that the clergy of the Middle Ages had done so.

The other legend was that the medieval churches were built for the glory of

God, and that all the workmen worked for the glory of God, and not at all for anyone else's glory: if there was a piece of work that would never be seen, they did it with more care than the pieces that would be seen.

One of the leading architects of the time, G. E. Street, refused to believe this. 'The workmen', he wrote, 'absolved themselves of all responsibility, worked the stones they were orderd to work, and ate their meals between times with the same absolute *sang froid* that marks their successors at the present day. They had no more pleasure in their work, no more originality in their way of doing it, than our workmen have at the present time, all the pretty fables to the contrary notwithstanding.' But most ecclesiologists were not willing to believe that.

It is true, of course, that an architectural profession did not exist then: nor did it for a very long time afterwards—not, in fact, until about the beginning of the eighteenth century. There was no class of men who sat an in office, and drew plans, without doing any of the practical work themselves. The Greek word *Tekton* means a craftsman, and an architect is a master-craftsman. The design was made by the master-mason, and the master-carpenter designed the roof. Sometimes the parish specified a particular church, or a particular part of a church, that they wanted copied. John Harvey has rescued the names of some of these master-masons, and it is interesting to know them; but most of them are rather shadowy people.

If the church was built by direct labour, the workmen were engaged and paid separately. If it was by contract, the master-craftsman would undertake to complete the building for a certain sum—though separate contracts might be made for each trade.

A few contracts survive:

At *Catterick,* Yorkshire, an agreement was made with Richard of Crakehall, in 1412, to build a new church (nave and aisles of four bays, and a chancel of three bays); and he was to finish the work in three years. If he did so, he was to receive 160 marks for the work, and an extra ten marks, and a gown.

For *Wyberton,* Lincolnshire, the actual contract has not survived, but it is known what it was, because there was a dispute about it afterwards. A bargain was made with Roger Denys, freemason, of London, on the feast of St Martin 1419, to build the nave, aisles, and steeple of the church in their entirety, of rough stones, without tabling or corbels, for 190 marks.

At *Fotheringhay*, Northamptonshire, a contract was made in 1434 for the making of 'a new body of a kirk joyning to the Quire of the College of Fodringhay', with aisles, a clearstory, and a steeple standing upon three strong and mighty arches at the west end. For this work William Horwood was to receive 450 marks; and there were severe penalties if he did not fulfil his part of the bargain.

A freemason worked with chisel and mallet on the finer freestone carvings: a rough mason shaped stones and laid them.

Stone might be quarried locally; but where there was none, it was bought from dealers. It might be worked, or partly worked, at the quarry from which it came. In the later years images, tombs, fonts, and so on were made in such places as Nottingham, Chellaston, York, Burton-on-Trent, Norwich, and London. There are products of the same workshops in many places, far apart, all looking exactly alike.

Undoubtedly there was some freedom for the carvers, but the idea that everyone just went ahead and did as they liked, doing everything out of their heads (building, as someone has said, as birds build their nests), and that the churches somehow got built, cannot be true.

It requires an effort of the imagination for some people to picture the churches as they were when they were first built. We think of them as old buildings, with a good deal of their outline and detail blurred by age and decay. We remember the illustrations in old parish magazines of the smock-clad rustic tottering towards an ivy-covered porch, supported by his granddaughter. And some will not go to see modern churches, simply because they are not old.

Obviously age has something to contribute to a building. But we must remember that there was a time when the scaffolding was only just down, and the church stood up new and clean, without any moss or ivy. It is necessary to picture that first. Then we can indulge in a dream of the interior. Let us suppose that we are visiting a church that has been newly built in the fifteenth century: there would be no point in going farther back and imagining the interior of a cold and dark Norman church.

The first thing that we notice is the colour. The walls are painted with saints and scenes from the life of our Lord, and with diaper in places on the pillars and arches. The windows have painted glass, and there is colour everywhere on the roofs and screens: red, white, green and gold.

The font is at the west end, coloured like all the rest of the church, with a cover that is kept locked. The water is only changed at Easter and Whitsun, and there is always a temptation to the parishioners to borrow some of it for medical or magical purposes.

Pulpits are becoming quite a regular feature of church furnishing; but the pulpit is quite modest and small.

At the east end of the nave is a most impressive erection. First there is the screen. At the top of it there is vaulting or a cove; and on top of that the loft, with a carved front. Above that is the rood: the figure of our Lord on the cross, with

St Mary and St John at the sides. This is brightly coloured, and may have clothes or shoes supplied by pious parishioners. Behind and above the rood, very often painted on boards filling the head of the chancel arch, is the Doom: our Lord on His throne, with the dead rising, and the good being sent to heaven, and the bad to hell.

Above the whole thing there is a canopy; and there may be a special window to light it.

The roods were specially obnoxious to the reformers later on. They said—not without reason—that they were objects of superstitious veneration. Images were treated as though they were real people.

All over the place are small altars, with lights burning in front of them, belonging to the various guilds of the parish.

The chancel is far less crowded than most chancels are nowadays. There is probably only one row of stalls, against the walls, and returned on the east side of the screen. There are, of course, no altar rails. The altar is vested, but there are no flowers and no cross on it: not more than two candles, and not always that. There is a low, carved reredos behind it, of wood, stone, or alabaster.

Now it is obvious that much of this has disappeared. England went through an iconoclastic period, and we have only the remains of what was once there. What is still left?

A majority of old churches still keeps the old font, and sometimes there is a cover, though this is often post-Reformation. This is no longer locked, as the water is renewed at every baptism.

Old seating is commonest in East Anglia, Devon, and Cornwall. The ends of the seats in East Anglia have a bunch of foliage, or some kind of emblem, on the top. Seats in the West Country are square-topped, and the ends are carved. The East Anglian benches are very uncomfortable; but our forefathers did not sit in church as much as we do.

At the ends of the aisles, and in the chancel, there is a piscina—a recess with a drain, which means that there was an altar there. There are often other small recesses, which were used as cupboards.

In the chancel, and occasionally elsewhere, there are the sedilia, on the south side: seats for the ministers during Mass.

Many screens survive, especially in the west. The loft has generally gone, though the stairs to it can often still be seen. A very few west galleries are the loft moved to the other end of the church. All ancient roods have gone.

There are remains of painting in many churches. A masonry pattern, with twists of conventional foliage, dates from the thirteenth century. There is no fixed scheme of paintings, except that the Doom was in, or over, the chancel arch, and was sometimes continued on the north and south walls. St Christopher is opposite the main doorway. St George with his dragon is common.

Occasionally there are pictures with a moral: the Wheel of Fortune, the Seven Deadly Sins, the Works of Mercy, or the Three Living and the Three Dead.

Glass is generally rather fragmentary. Thirteenth-century glass is either grisaille, or figures and scenes in roundels. In the fourteenth century, there are standing figures, generally S-shaped, under tall canopies. Fifteenth-century figures stand upright. Canopies are smaller, and have a conventional array of pinnacles and crockets.

Yellow stain came in during the fourteenth century. As time went on there was improvement in the making of glass: it becomes thinner, the surface is more regular, and the colours are smoother.

Old glass is often to be found in the tracery of a window: it has remained there when the rest has gone. (The same thing happened in raids in the last war.)

Monuments remain in large numbers. The coffin-lid type did not last much beyond the thirteenth century. Thirteenth-century effigies are usually placed low down, and are rather flat.

Later, effigies are placed on an oblong stone chest: the sides—or one side, if it is against a wall—have figures in niches, called weepers. It is disappointing to learn that the effigies are hardly ever portraits: figures of a knight and lady were ordered from the monumental masons, and far more trouble was taken with the armour and the clothes than with the faces.

The earliest brasses are of the second half of the thirteenth century. Fifteenth- and early sixteenth-century brasses are very common. The workmanship deteriorates as time goes on: the later ones are coarsely cut, with attempts at shading.

THE SIXTEENTH AND
SEVENTEENTH CENTURIES

❋ ❋

England had far more than its fair share of religious troubles in the sixteenth and seventeenth centuries, and times of religious controversy are not times of church building. The guilds and chantries were dissolved in 1547–8, and those sources of benefactions came to an end. In any case, the country had all the churches that it needed, and far too many in some places. There are several tiny villages in Norfolk that were divided into two parishes, and had two churches: even two in the same churchyard. Many of these churches have disappeared in the last 300 years, but there are still very many, and enough to be a serious embarrassment to those who have to keep them in repair.

So from the middle of the sixteenth century to the middle of the seventeenth there is very little to report. But something ought to be said about the changes in internal arrangement at this time.

In the reign of Henry VIII there was practically no change. In the short reign of Edward VI, when the English services were introduced, there was much destruction, owing more to greed than to religious zeal. During Mary's reign the Latin services were restored, and there was some attempt to make good the damage that had been done. In the reign of Elizabeth I there was a good deal of unofficial destruction by the Puritan party. The Nonconformists at the time had not separated themselves from the Church of England: they stayed in it, but refused to conform to its rules, in the hope of bringing about a more thorough Reformation. Elizabeth, who liked a decent and ceremonious worship, issued several proclamations to stop the destruction. The stone altars were being removed, if they had not already been, in favour of wooden ones. An injunction of 1559 said that it did not much matter whether the holy table was of stone or of wood, but that if a new wooden one was made it must be vested properly and stand at the east end. At the time of Communion it could be moved to the most convenient place in the chancel, but it must be put back at the east end afterwards.

Roods and lofts were taken down, but the screen was to remain. Every church was to have a pulpit. Wall paintings were whitewashed over, and the walls were to be painted with texts. The painted glass windows were to remian.

It was not a very religious time, and many churches were in poor condition. (But it is only fair to say that many of them had been dilapidated before the religious changes began. The visitations of the Archdeaconry of Oxford in the early sixteenth century, which were printed some years ago, show a shocking state of affairs in many parishes.) But it was not as bad a time as some have attempted to make out.

The church building that was done was in ordinary late (the Victorians said Debased) Perpendicular.

But new ideas were beginning to come in, though at first they appear mainly in monuments, and in details or woodwork. Buildings were still in the late Gothic tradition, with new details grafted on. This was the time of the Renaissance: the renewal of interest in the life, the literature, and the architecture of ancient Rome. Roman architecture was a coarser and more flexible version of Greek, with the addition of the arch, which the Greeks did not use.

The essentials were the columns; which supported the entablature, which consists of three parts—the architrave, the frieze, and the cornice. The writers of the Renaissance worked it all out into a system, with the details and the proportions of the five Orders—Tuscan, Doric, Ionic, Corinthian, and Composite—all classified.

The Renaissance had been flourishing in Italy for a hundred years, but the new fashion reached England at second or third hand, chiefly through books of engravings made in the Low Countries, which gave pictures of ornament—often very ugly and debased—which was alleged to be Classical, and which Englishmen received with enthusiasm, imagining it to be the real thing.

The first Englishman to design a really Classical building was Inigo Jones (1573–1651), and the first building was the Banqueting House in Whitehall (which we may just count as a church, as it was used for a time as a royal chapel). The first place of worship was the Queen's Chapel (now the Chapel of Marlborough House). And the first parish church was St Paul's, Covent Garden, which was finished in 1631. It was burned down in 1795, but was rebuilt nearly as it was. It has a Tuscan portico at the east. The rest of the church was always very simple; but it originally had a painted ceiling, and other decorations, which are there no longer.

But there is nothing else like St Paul's. During the reign of Charles I, under the influence of Archbishop Laud, a good deal was done to repair and refit the old churches. But the few new churches that were built are certainly not Renaissance.

Groombridge, Kent, is traditional. St John's, Leeds, is the same, but it is fitted with an imposing array of woodwork in the new fashion. Leighton Bromswold, Huntingdonshire, is also late Perpendicular, though the rather later tower has round arches. St Catherine Cree, in the City, is a very odd church: partly Classical, but with a Gothic vault, and an east end which is a miniature reproduction of old St Paul's.

During the Civil War and the Commonwealth there was naturally very little church building. An almost incredible piece of Gothic survival is the church (really a private chapel) of Staunton Harold, Leicestershire, begun in 1653, which is Perpendicular throughout, except for the west doorway, which has Flemish ornament. Plaxtol is a Kentish church built during the Commonwealth.

Then, in 1660, Charles II came into his own again, and the Church of England came back, too. A considerable amount of repair and refitting was done afterwards, and there are a good many fonts dated about this time.

THE CHURCHES OF SIR CHRISTOPHER WREN

In 1666 the City of London was burned down. Three surveyors were appointed for the rebuilding, of whom Wren was one. Sir Christopher Wren (1632–1723), who had been born and brought up in a Laudian High Church family, was well known as a mathematician and a scientist. He was appointed to succeed to the position of surveyor of the Royal Works before he had designed a single building: his first buildings were begun in 1662. He was consulted about the rebuilding of St Paul's after the Fire, and from 1670 fifty-one of the churches in the City were being rebuilt.

Wren's problem was to design churches which should be suitable to the Prayer Book ideal of common worship. (It is doing less than justice to the churchmanship of the time to suggest, as is so often done, that hearing the sermon was all that mattered. There were many books written about the English Liturgy in the seventeenth century, which explained the services, often with great learning, expounding the meaning of each several prayer, and its relation to the rest. Congregations were expected to follow the services with intelligence and devotion, not merely to sit back and wait for the sermon.) He had also to fit neatly planned churches into the confined, and often oddly-shaped, sites on which the destroyed churches had stood. Sometimes, where there was room, he used the traditional nave-and-aisles plan. Sometimes he used the Greek cross—a square containing a cross with arms of equal length, with or without a central dome. One or two churches were rectangles with a single aisle. Some were of an exceptional shape, such as St Benet Fink, which was a decagon with an elliptical dome in the middle. Generally, there was an emphasis on the centre, and the plan was a geometrical figure.

Wren's steeples are all his own: they had no Classical precedent, and some of them are a Renaissance version of the spires of the Middle Ages. They were designed to be seen above the housetops, and they gave London a character all of its own. The pity is that so many of them have gone, and that so many of those that remain have been swamped by large recent buildings.

The fittings of Wren's churches—the plasterwork, woodwork, altarpieces, and so on—are, generally speaking, not Wren's. They were paid for by the parishes, which made bargains directly with the workmen. Wren himself was correct and Classical: these are exuberant, and sometimes rather vulgar. It is curious that the fittings have been considered essential to Wren, and that when people have tried to reproduce what they call the Wren style, these are the things that they have copied.

There are a few churches like those in the City outside London. But the City churches really stand in a class by themselves, and they were not, generally speaking, models likely to be imitated elsewhere. The churches of Wren that had the most influence were the few that he built on unencumbered sites, particularly St James's, Piccadilly. St James's had to be built fairly cheaply to hold a large congregation in a growing new district. Wren himself has given us his thoughts about it. A church, he wrote, should be large, but not too large. 'The Romanists indeed may build larger Churches: it is enough if they hear the murmur of the Mass, and see the elevation of the Host: but ours are to be fitted as auditories.' He had tried, at St James's, to build a church in which 2,000 people could hear distinctly, and see the preacher. The whole church, though very broad, and with the middle nave arched up, had no walls with a second order, but the whole roof rested on the pillars, and so did the galleries. He thought that it was beautiful and convenient, and the cheapest of any form that he could invent.

What he had done was to make a two-storied church: not just a church with galleries in it, but a church with each story complete in itself, and marked in the architecture. This became the usual form for large town churches for the next 150 years.

NONCONFORMIST CHURCHES

There are a few earlier chapels, but the building of places of worship for Nonconformists really began after Charles II's Declaration of Indulgence in 1672, and William III's Toleration Act in 1688. Most of the early chapels were very humble, but there are some—such as the Old Meeting at Norwich (1693), and the Friar Street Unitarian Chapel at Ipswich (1700)—that are well designed and fitted with admirable woodwork. The pulpit is often placed in the middle of one of the longer sides of the chapel, with the seats facing inward towards it: the same arrangement as can be seen in the older Presbyterian churches in Scotland.

THE
EIGHTEENTH CENTURY

❀ ❀

THE FIFTY NEW CHURCHES

In 1711 an Act was passed for building fifty new churches in London and the suburbs. St Paul's had been built by a tax on coal, and this was continued for the benefit of the new churches.

The Commissioners appointed under the Act made careful inquiries in each London parish about the population and the church accommodation, and a large number of parishes applied to have their churches rebuilt out of the funds and counted in the fifty.

In fact, nothing like fifty were built. When Queen Anne died, and George I came to the throne, there was, under a Whig Government, a lessening of interest in the scheme, and finally it lapsed altogether. The Commissioners had models made for the proposed churches—which were kept at Westminster Abbey, but have disappeared. Wren gave them a memorandum on the subject, and so did Sir John Vanbrugh.

The surveyors appointed to design and supervise the churches were Nicholas Hawksmoor (1661–1736) and William Dickinson (c. 1671–1725)—who retired, and was succeeded by James Gibbs (1682–1752). In 1715 Gibbs was dismissed, as being a Roman Catholic and a Tory, and was succeeded by John James (c. 1672–1746).

Hawksmoor designed the greatest number of churches: St George in the East; St George's, Bloomsbury; St Alphege's, Greenwich; St Anne's, Limehouse; St Mary Woolnoth (in the City), and Christchurch, Spitalfields, are his, and he helped with others.

Hawksmoor had been Wren's assistant for some time, and had been developing a baroque[1] style of his own. He had never been to Rome, but he had a great interest in anything Roman, and especially in the less well known Roman buildings. His churches are solemn, heavy, and monumental.

[1] An exuberant Roman style, with plenty of movement—as opposed to correct Classical architecture according to the rules.

Thomas Archer (*c.* 1668–1743) was another baroque architect: he designed St John's, Westminster, St Paul's, Deptford, and (outside London) St Philip's, Birmingham. James Gibbs produced one church for the Commission: the beautiful and elegant St Mary-le-Strand, the result of his studies in Rome.

John James designed St George's, Hanover Square, a church of the type of St James's, Piccadilly, but with a west portico, with a small tower above.

OTHER EIGHTEENTH-CENTURY CHURCHES

The work of the Commission came to an end, and all the rest of the church building of the century was done by the parishes, or by private individuals. And baroque soon became unpopular, and the Palladian[1] fashion took its place (at any rate among the Men of Taste: echoes of the fifty churches may be found in the works of the provincial architects).

The church that had the greatest influence was designed by one of the Commissioners' architects—James Gibbs—but was not one of the fifty: St Martin-in-the-Fields.

Gibbs made more than one design for this important church. The first was thought too expensive: the second was the church as it was built. It is more or less like Wren's larger churches, such as St James's, Piccadilly, but it has large single columns, with the galleries built up against them, not a double order—one supporting the galleries, and one rising from them. The steeple is built inside the west end of the church, with the portico in front of it. Fault has often been found with this combination of portico and steeple, but it was often imitated.

The influence of St Martin's was very widespread, not only because it was so important a church, but also because Gibbs produced a book which contained drawings of it, together with various alternative designs for the steeple, which, as he said, could be reproduced without difficulty by the ordinary builder. The book must have been taken to America at once, and several American churches reproduce the whole, or part, of St Martin's. Quebec Cathedral, the first cathedral to be built in Canada, was based on it: and Gibbs-like churches are to be found as far away as India.

The inside of St Peter's, Vere Street, Marylebone, is a simpler and smaller version of the body of St Martin's. Another well-known church by Gibbs is All Saints', Derby, where there were no galleries. The builder of All Saints' was Francis Smith of Warwick (1672–1738), one of a firm of master builders who were responsible for several large and handsome churches in the Midlands, all much alike.

[1] Andrea Palladio (1518–80), architect and writer, who gave rules for the correct proportions, etc., of the Orders.

The eighteenth century was a time of regular and steady church building. Some of it was done by benefactors. The local nobleman or squire would often offer to take down the old decayed church, and build one more convenient and handsome. There are many of these hidden away in quiet parishes, near the big house.

But most of it was done by the parishes. It was, and still is, the business of the churchwardens and (at that time) of the vestry to provide accommodation for all the parishioners and to keep the church in repair. And it was possible then—as it has not been for nearly a hundred years—to levy a church rate on all the householders. If this did not produce enough, the parish would apply for a brief—an appeal to other parishes, either throughout the country or in particular counties.

When a church was out of repair and was rebuilt it was, in the country places, usually rebuilt smaller than before. There was no thought of size in itself as being to the glory of God; and nothing now went on in the church—except sometimes for the vestry meetings—apart from the services, so that there was no need to have much space. The straightforward idea of the time was to produce a decent, sound, and elegant building, which would hold the parishioners, and not cost more money than it was possible to raise.

As the population grew in London and other big towns the old churches were first crammed with pews and galleries, and then rebuilt, if it became impossible to fit in any more seating. A good many chapels of ease were built, or hired: big London parishes such as St Martin-in-the-Fields had several. They were not consecrated, and could be given up if they were no longer required. There is much to be said for this: the custom in the later part of the next century was to build permanent churches, and to give them parishes of their own as soon as possible. This has often turned out to be an embarrassment, as the population of London is always shifting, and many of these Victorian parishes have been left stranded. The chapels in an eighteenth-century parish were kept going as long as they were needed, and could be disposed of without difficulty.

New parishes were rare: to make a new parish meant creating a civil as well as an ecclesiastical unit, and an Act of Parliament was necessary for this. It was not until the nineteenth century that a parish could be made that was ecclesiastical alone.

About planning there is not much to be said. The large churches were of the Wren-Gibbs type; the smaller ones had a nave with or without aisles and tower; and chancels were usually short. The chancel was the altar-place: what we should call the sanctuary. A clear space was sometimes left in front of it for the communicants to stand in, but there was no thought of making a chancel long simply for length's sake. Indeed, in recasting old churches, the chancel was often reduced. In a small parish, where there were not many communicants, it was made only as long as was required to accommodate them.

The fittings of an eighteenth-century church are important: more trouble was often taken over them than with the church itself. Fittings of the same sort were introduced, if the parish could afford them, into ancient churches.

To begin with, there were the pews. Every rate-paying parishioner was entitled to a pew for himself and his family. If he liked to make one for himself, and save expense to the parish, he was welcome to do so. But the churchwardens and vestries liked to have the pews uniform, and payments for repewing in a uniform manner occur constantly in churchwardens' accounts. The pews were almost always box pews with doors, often beautifully made.

There were usually galleries, if there was not room on the floor: these, too, could be erected by particular people, but were made uniform if possible. A west gallery was practically universal for the singers, and the organ if there was one.

The floor was, if possible, paved. Often the sanctuary was more elaborately done, with squares of black and white marble, or stone with black marble dots.

The roof was always ceiled, sometimes with a cove, and more or less elaborate plaster work. An unceiled roof was thought to look mean: if there was no ceiling, the archdeacon would give the order to put one up, and the churchwardens would promise to do so as soon as they could. A brass chandelier (a branch or spider), hanging from a rose in the centre, was very common.

The pulpit, usually of the three-decker type, was often, in small churches, half-way down one side. Some pulpits and canopies are beautifully inlaid. The pulpit was adorned with cushion and hangings.

The altar was enclosed in rails, projecting or square in plan. It was small in size, and covered with a fringed velvet cloth. There was, if possible, an altar-piece: a Classical background of pillars and pediment, often enclosing paintings, and almost always including the Creed, Lord's Prayer, and Ten Commandments.

An eighteenth-century church, or a Georgianized old church, which has been left alone, always looks neat and furnished. Unfortunately, there are few that have been left as they were. In many cases they have been reseated, and the galleries and ceilings have been taken down; choir stalls have been inserted, and a general attempt has been made to twist them into the semblance of a Gothic or Byzantine church. But an unaltered interior of this century always looks gentlemanly and civilized. There is a good example at Langton by Spilsby, in Lincolnshire. The building is very plain, but the furniture is magnificent. A church like this makes one realize how much has been lost from so many eighteenth-century churches.

Gothic continued to be used fairly regularly through the century. Sometimes it is simply Gothic survival. But towards the end of the century there was a definite feeling in the minds of some people that a church ought to be Gothic, and there were attempts to design something that was supposed to recall an old church.

There was not, as we said at the beginning, the slightest understanding of the real nature of Gothic, and all that was done was to point the windows slightly, and sometimes to give them mullions and some elementary tracery, and to substitute battlements and pinnacles for a balustrade.

One of the earliest and most astonishing efforts is Tetbury church, Gloucestershire, by Francis Hiorne (1744–89). It is lit by enormous traceried windows, and divided into nave and aisles by the slimmest of iron columns, cased in wood, and covered with a plaster vault. The admirable box pews remain, and much of the beauty of the interior depends on them. The altar-piece, of normal eighteenth-century type, except for a few pinnacles and crockets, has lately been replaced. It is in every way a splendid church; but the nineteenth-century critics, while giving credit for good intentions, would have said that it was not really Gothic: it is a large church of the usual eighteenth-century plan, with Gothic instead of Classical details.

In the latter part of the century, besides the growing interest in Gothic, there was the influence of Adam and Wyatt, who broke away from the scholarship of the approved writers and introduced a lighter, more ornamental style. There was also the growing influence of Greece. Travellers began to explore Greece, and to study her ancient buildings—the origin of Roman architecture—and to realize that they were of a simpler and purer kind than they had been used to. Before the end of the century one or two churches had been built that showed Greek influence.

It might also be mentioned that the importation of timber from the Baltic made it possible to roof a larger area than before without the help of pillars, so that large churches could now be built which were a large hall, unbroken by pillars above the galleries; which was less interesting, but cheaper.

NONCONFORMIST CHURCHES

The later eighteenth-century chapels are much the same as the plainer Anglican chapels and the few that were built by the Roman Catholics: rectangular, galleried, and ceiled, with large, round-headed windows.

The earliest Methodist meeting-houses (John Wesley insisted that they were not to be called chapels, but they were) are similar: Wesley said that they should be plain. One or two are of the octagonal form which he preferred. Wesley's Chapel in the City Road (1777–8) is a handsome and dignified building.

ROMAN CATHOLIC CHURCHES

Some of the repressive laws against Roman Catholics in England were repealed in 1778, and further relief was given in 1791. The churches built after this were modest, chapel-like buildings, of which a few remain. Some were more ambitiously Classical, and some attempts were made at Gothic.

THE
NINETEENTH CENTURY

❋ ❋

THE CHURCH BUILDING COMMISSION

The pace of church building slowed down during the latter part of the eighteenth century and the beginning of the nineteenth, the period of the Napoleonic Wars. But the population was growing, and the new towns, the result of the Industrial Revolution, were growing up.

After the war, in 1818, the Church Building Society was founded; and in the same year Parliament voted a sum of money for the building of new churches, and set up a commission to deal with the matter. Another grant was made in 1824, and that was the last time that the Church of England received any help from the State.

The new churches are generally known as the Commissioners' Churches (the name Waterloo Churches is a mistake): there were many others that received grants later on. They are, naturally, mostly in London and the industrial areas, and a large proportion is in Yorkshire.

There is not much to be said about these churches in the matter of planning. The aim of the Commissioners was to make room for as many people as possible for a reasonable sum—though as a matter of fact some of the larger churches were decidedly expensive. The designs were either Greek or Gothic: in either case, some kind of tower or belfry was provided, to make it clear that this was a church and not a chapel. (Objection was soon to be made to this by the ecclesiologists, who said that attention should be paid to the east end of a church, not the west: what made a building church-like was a properly designed chancel, not a display in the facade.)

Several of the Gothic churches were designed by Thomas Rickman, the writer on Gothic architecture: they are certainly more correct in their detail than those of most other architects of the time, but he was not a medievalist, and had no objection to using cast iron for window tracery and other features.

The plan of one of his churches is, on paper, much the same as that of a fifteenth-century church with aisles and chapels: but the whole layout of the interior is

40

different. It is planned to hold a hypothetical congregation of so many, and the whole of the interior space is used for that: none for the subsidiary altars and chantries of the Middle Ages. The side walls are higher than fifteenth-century walls would have been, and the tower is slimmer than a fifteenth-century tower: the angles between it and the body of the church are filled with porches, which also contain the stairs to the galleries. The whole thing is rather stiff and formal. The general appearance is reasonably correct, but the details have an unmistakably early nineteenth-century character, which it is easier to recognize than to describe.

Churches like this do not deserve all the hard things that have been said about them. Many have considerable dignity. But they are hardly lovable.

TRUE PRINCIPLES

Gothic has been thought of so far chiefly as ornament: it was not realized that the essence of Gothic is in construction. Pointed arches are not only beautiful, they are more secure than semicircular arches. And the development of Gothic is obviously connected with the development of vaulting, and of buttresses, so that, as time went on, there could be less wall and more window. This had not been understood, or at any rate not thought important. The man who first preached it was Pugin.

Augustus Welby Northmore Pugin (1812-1852), the son of a French refugee, was a small, dark, energetic man, who burned himself out in a few years, and died insane at the age of 40. His writings are vigorous, entertaining, unfair, and provocative: he meant to annoy people, and he certainly succeeded.

The heart of Pugin's gospel was that there should be no features about a building that are not necessary for convenience, construction, or propriety: and that all ornament should consist of the enrichment of the essential construction of the building.

He does not make it clear what he means by convenience or propriety: but he leaves no doubt at all that Gothic is the only style that has the necessary qualities.

And it has another justification as well: that it, and it alone, is Christian architecture. Pugin had been brought up as a Nonconformist, but soon joined the Roman Catholic Church, where he was not much appreciated. With the usual churches, and church fittings, of his day, Roman and non-Roman, he was disgusted. But he had a vision of the Middle Ages, when England was a Christian country, and all her architecture was Christian. There were beautiful cities, undefiled by industry, peopled with pious citizens. He pictured noble churches, with soaring spires, and niches filled with figures of saints. In imagination he entered their portals and gazed at the twinkling points of light and the rich colours of the glass. There were altars, and rich screens, and metal-work, and tiles, and priests in beautiful vestments, and acolytes in albs. And he could reproduce the dream, on paper, and contrast it with the mean and sordid and sham building of his own day.

When he came to translating it into fact, he was not so successful, and there was only one church of his with which he was really satisfied: St Augustine's, Ramsgate.

But things could not be the same after Pugin as they had been before. What he called true principles of Gothic came to be accepted: and also the doctrine that Gothic is Christian architecture.

But the influence of Pugin on the Church of England has been exaggerated. Ideas similar to his were being discussed in Anglican circles: but they arose more or less independently, and the people who developed them were a great deal more scholarly than he was. Before long, they were inclined to say, 'Poor Pugin. He did a good work, and we are grateful for his writings. But he has made no progress, and he keeps repeating himself. And whatever he may say about construction, he spends too much of his time in designing ornament—which is easy to do, but does not get us much further.'

Ecclesiology—the word that the Anglican churchmen invented—means the study of the church building, of the ornaments and fittings of it, and of the worship that goes on in it. The main doctrines of the Ecclesiologists were these:

(1) Gothic is Christian architecture. But any kind of Gothic would not do. Early English was undeveloped, Perpendicular was decadent. Gothic at its best was Decorated (or Middle-Pointed, as the ecclesiologists preferred to call it). At first they said that it reached its climax about the middle of the fourteenth century: later they said about the beginning of it. But at any rate there was a point at which it reached its highest development: they must take it up from there, learn how to do it properly, and then go on from there.

(2) They shared with Pugin the belief that honest construction was necessary to Gothic, and that materials must be real: stone and wood, not artificial stone or plaster.

(3) They believed also, as Pugin did, that an architect should be a Christian and a churchman, and that if he was he would be able to infuse into his designs a Christian spirit that would not otherwise be there. If possible, he should design only churches, and such buildings as schools and colleges. Railroad stations, workhouses, etc., would have a corrupting effect.

(4) But correct style was not enough: there must also be correct arrangement. And in this matter the ecclesiologists waged unceasing war on the church planning that had been customary for so long. There must be a good-sized chancel, and the priest must have his stall there—not outside in the nave. The choir also should be there—not in a gallery at the west. The three-decker pulpit must go, and the pulpit

must be low and unobtrusive. The lessons should be read from a lectern (or lettern, as they preferred to spell it). Box pews and galleries must go, and all seats must be low and open. The font should have a cover and stand at the west end.

They were so successful in teaching this that it has become until recently practically universal. It has, in fact, become the standard Anglican arrangement, and there are very few churches left that have anything else. The fact is that the old arrangements, though not in themselves necessarily un-churchlike, had by then become old-fashioned and were associated in people's minds with the easygoing ways of the Georgian era, that were obviously not good enough for the new situation in the 40s. Many churchmen who would not go the whole way with the ecclesiologists were as sure as they were about this, and the old arrangements rapidly disappeared almost altogether.

CHURCH RESTORATION

From the 40s onward, under ecclesiological influence, most of the ancient churches in the country were restored.

Restoration is not the same thing as repair. Repairs had been done all through the eighteenth century. Sometimes—especially in areas where there was building stone and a tradition of masoncraft—these had been done so carefully, and in so traditional a manner, that it is not possible now to distinguish the work from the original. But more often they were done in a way that altered the appearance of the church. We should say that they made it attractive and picturesque: but the Victorians did not think so. Most eighteenth-century vestries could see no point in reproducing what seemed to them foolish and fantastic stonework in windows, and preserving ornamental features that had become dilapidated. They would patch and buttress the walls with brick, insert large round-headed windows with clear glass, make dormers in the roof to light the gallery; and generally make a patchwork, such as can still be seen at Esher, Surrey, and Minstead, Hampshire. We think it pleasant to look at; but to churchmen a hundred years ago it appeared simply as mean debasement, fit only to be removed as quickly as possible.

When in the eighteenth century the inside of the church had been made neat and uniform, and accommodation had been provided for all the parishioners, and three-decker, panelling, and altar-piece had been erected, the church looked handsome, and satisfied everyone very well. No one could say that it looked as it had in the Middle Ages. But why should it? There had been changes in worship, and this was an old church adapted to the worship of the time.

But it was beginning to be felt very strongly in the 40s that the ordinary ways of worship were incapable of meeting the new needs of the day. The old parish life, too, was breaking down; and it had broken down completely in the big new towns. The assumption that all householders were members of the Church of England, and that all would pay their church rates, was very wide of the mark in Birmingham or Manchester. And many churchmen were beginning to see the whole system as a positive hindrance to church life. Voluntary giving must take the place of the church rate, and the rented pew must give way to free and open sittings. This was not an entirely new idea: the Church Building Society had from the beginning insisted that some, at least, of the seats in the churches to which it gave grants must be free. But the idea was gathering momentum, and obviously if it were accepted it would lead to the complete rearrangement of the interiors of the churches.

The ideal, then, of the ecclesiologists was to remove all pews and galleries, and the three-decker pulpit, and rearrange the interior correctly, with low, open seats, and the chancel brought back into use.

But it was not possible to rearrange the inside and leave the fabric untouched. At the very least, the clearing-out process would involve the removal of projecting family pews, the outside steps that led to galleries, and the dormer windows in the roof. But the removal of all this furniture, and of the plaster ceilings, would almost always reveal decay that had not been noticed before. And not only repair, but some replacement would be necessary.

There were very few churches that had all their ancient features intact. Destruction in the sixteenth century, and in the Great Rebellion, had affected many of them; and seventeenth- and eighteenth-century repairs and neatening had removed many others. There were, in fact, many churches that had lost all visible ancient features, except for the walls. What was to be done with them?

There was not much difficulty if a church was all of one period. But most churches are not: they are an agglomeration of parts, dating from different centuries. What, in such cases, was it that ought to be restored?

The ecclesiologists distinguished three points of view among themselves.

The Conservatives said, 'Restore a church as it is.'

The Destructives said, 'It is legitimate to remove something, if something better is put in its place. Debased work may always be removed in favour of something in a purer style.'

The Eclectics said, 'There is no general rule: it depends on the church.'

But everyone was agreed, in the early days of the movement, that if there were new additions to be made, or if the whole, or part, of a church had to be rebuilt, then the best style must be used.

The restorers have been blamed for faking old work, but there is no need to worry too much about that. Nineteenth-century Gothic has something about it that makes it look different from medieval work. Even when it is several hundred years older and has weathered, most of it will probably still look like what it is.

By about 1880, most churches had been restored—some badly, some well. There is no doubt that many restorations succeeded in making charming and attractive churches out of dull and undistinguished ones. There is also no doubt that some churches were spoiled.

By that time a reaction was setting in, and William Morris and his followers were preaching anti-restoration doctrine. They said that restoration had taken away the texture and charm of many churches, and that what was needed was not restoration but preservation.

That is generally accepted now: even if we had the money, we should not do as the Victorians did. We are Conservatives, and try to keep the character of each church, without trying to make it into something that it never was. (The danger now is that good Victorian work may be removed—which is as unjustifiable as the Victorian removal of good Georgian work.)

NINETEENTH-CENTURY ANGLICAN CHURCHES

Now that the ecclesiologists' ideal church has been described, it only remains to be said that it was sometimes realized almost completely. The churches, for instance, of R. C. Carpenter (1812–55) are almost as good as they could be, in this kind.

A criticism of the town churches of this time that could be made, and was made, is that they are not, in fact, town churches at all, but country churches transplanted from Northamptonshire or Lincolnshire. It is indeed in the villages that such churches appear at their best: there they are just right. But it was realized that a more suitable type of church would have to be devised for the towns.

It is very wide of the mark to say that the nineteenth-century architects and churchmen were interested only in copying. Ecclesiology did not stand still, and it was only for a very few years that the original gospel of the ecclesiologists was held without alteration. They realized that they must re-learn the elements of Gothic, and train workmen who would be able to work naturally in it. But it was certainly not enough to copy: the nineteenth century must develop a Gothic of its own. This was also a time of great expansion overseas: and, while English fourteenth-century Gothic could be used in New Zealand or Australia, it could obviously not be transported to India or Africa without alteration. (Sometimes it was; but it was not very suitable. The exiled Englishman might like to have something to remind him of the village church at home, but large windows would make him uncomfortably hot. It was clearly advisable to think out a different type of church for the tropics.)

The original ideal church had been completely English; but was it not possible to learn from other countries? The answer was Yes, and architects began to travel abroad, and to return with new ideas, about both materials and style.

English churches generally have walls of plain stone, but there are some that have varied colours, in bands, or round the arches. And there was far more of that in Italy. Why not introduce constructional colour into churches? There were various English stones that could be used, and some marbles and granite could be polished, and used for shafts and columns. And why not brick? The earliest ecclesiologists had disliked it; but there were many brick Gothic churches abroad, and even a few in England. Bricks could easily be made in all kinds of colours, and it was not really possible to say that brick was not a real material.

The first church in which this was put into practice was All Saints', Margaret Street, which was undertaken as the Ecclesiological Society's model church—though it was a great shock to many ecclesiologists when they saw it. William Butterfield (1814–1900) was an architect of great power and originality. His churches are certainly honest in their construction, and generally austere, ascetic, and angular—like Butterfield himself. Sometimes he failed to do himself justice; but even in his poorer churches there is something of the tough, take-it-or-leave-it spirit of the more aggressive High Churchmen of the time. (His seats, for instance, are almost fanatically low, and uncomfortable to sit in; but kneeling is easy.)

All Saints' was obviously a town church, and so was his other famous London church, St Alban's, Holborn. St Matthias', Stoke Newington, was more or less in the country when it was built, but Butterfield designed it to fit in with, and to dominate, the streets of small houses that were being built around it.

In the matter of style, architects began to borrow from Italy and France, particularly France. French thirteenth-century work was more solid and robust than English, and it kept the square abacus for longer. It struck some of the younger architects that here was something more satisfactory than the pretty English fourteenth-century work, with its curves and naturalistic carvings: it had more vigour and go.

One of the dominating figures in nineteenth-century church building was G. E. Street (1824–81). His earliest work is ordinary but good ecclesiological Gothic; but he did more than anyone else to introduce the foreign element. It was not simply copying: he developed a style that was all his own. It had many imitators, and he himself tended to leave it behind later on. But his churches of the later 50s and 60s are characteristic, and easily recognizable. They have some constructional polychrome, the square abacus, deliberately coarse and large-scale foliage, an almost entire elimination of mouldings, except for chamfers; and windows that looked (people said) as though they had been cut out of pastry. In one or two of his town churches he experimented with a plan that would be more

46

suitable to common worship than the usual English medieval one: a wide nave, in which all the congregation could be together, and narrow passage aisles. But he was also a country architect, and some of his village churches are among his most pleasant works. At his best, he was almost the ideal Victorian architect: devout, hard-working, and—in spite of his foreign importations—extremely English.

By the 70s the foreign Gothic fashion was coming to an end, and there was often a return to English: sometimes earlier, and sometimes later, than the original Middle-Pointed. Three architects deserve mention.

J. L. Pearson, after his early Middle-Pointed period, had a short French Gothic phase. His fine church of St Peter, Vauxhall—exactly what a Victorian High church in a poor district ought to be—has French detail; but he soon returned to an English thirteenth-century style. He was almost the only nineteenth-century architect who always, if possible, gave a stone vault to his churches; and no one else could match his skill in constructing vaults. It is not likely that there will ever again be churches like his: large, lofty, expensive, and devout churches such as St Michael's, Croydon, St Augustine's, Kilburn, and St John's, Upper Norwood. But we must admire the generosity and self-sacrifice of the later nineteenth-century churchmen who were convinced that this was the kind of church that they ought to have to worship in. This was indeed building to the glory of God.

G. F. Bodley (1827–1907) went through a somewhat similar development. His earliest churches are French, but he soon took up a fourteenth-century style, rather later than that which the ecclesiologists had at first approved, and developed it to a refinement that medieval Gothic had never had. The interior of a Bodley church is light and delicate, with carved screens, and, if possible, a carved and gilded wooden altar-piece. He was fond of wagon roofs painted in green and gold, and a similar colour scheme on the walls. Sometimes he carries refinement a little too far; but his churches must have been a great relief after some of the crude and aggressive foreign Gothic churches built just before his time: and indeed they were still being built during it.

Sir A. W. Blomfield (1829–99) began with a French style, and then became rather dull. He was a great producer of suburban churches in areas that were being developed in the 80s.

The most prolific of all the church architects of the nineteenth century was Sir Gilbert Scott (1811–78), who is said to have built, or restored, over 700 churches after the mid 40s. Scott was the complete Eminent Victorian. He had risen from a comparatively humble origin by ambition and hard work. He was genuinely religious, and had no doubt that he was divinely led to his position of eminence.

He considered himself to be an interpreter of the Gothic Revival to the ordinary person: he gave people what they wanted, and that is why he was so successful. The ecclesiologists had been too churchy and scholarly for the ordinary man: Scott was a mediator, who carried out their principles in a modified way. He had been converted, in his younger days, to a belief in chancels and in real materials, and he accepted, in theory, their doctrine of a style of a certain date, which should be the starting-point of the Revival. He accepted also the principle of borrowing from abroad. But he was never carried away too much by anything. His accomplishment varied a good deal: if he was interested, and took trouble, he did well, but he turned out a good deal that was mediocre.

One of his sons, George Gilbert II (1839–97), designed a few very good churches at the end of the century—two of which, St Agnes', Kennington, and All Hallows', Southwark—were unfortunately destroyed by bombing. Another son, John Oldrid (1842–1913), designed a great many churches, that do not, to us, seem very attractive. But they may come into fashion one day.

There were, of course, hundreds of other architects who designed churches in different parts of the country.

And there were the local architects, whose work is more or less confined to a certain area: Fowler of Louth; Kirk of Sleaford; Chatwin of Birmingham; Bidlake of Birmingham; Ferguson of Carlisle; Douglas of Chester; Medland and Henry Taylor of Manchester; Hodgson Fowler of Durham and Yorkshire, and many others. Their work is similar, more or less, to that of the few well-known architects that we have mentioned; and often just as good.

And, lest anyone should imagine that the ecclesiologists carried all before them, it must be added that there were always those who refused to conform: those whom Goodhart Rendel called the Rogues. Sir William Tite's church at Gerrards Cross was a most impressive protest against ecclesiology; and architects such as E. B. Lamb and Bassett Keeling did their best to break as many as possible of the ecclesiological rules.

ROMAN CATHOLIC CHURCHES

Pugin, after his conversion in 1834, bitterly attacked the architecture and the liturgical arrangements with which English Roman Catholics had hitherto been quite content: rectangular Italianate chapels without screens, tawdry altars, and debased vestments were a disgrace to the Church, and those who were satisfied with them were hardly true Catholics at all. A church ought to be Gothic, correctly arranged, and provided with screens (this was essential); and the altars and vestments must be medieval in design.

He was able to build several churches that were almost the real thing: some of his smaller churches are simple and charming. And there are two in which he was able to do as he liked: St Giles, Cheadle, Staffordshire, built at the cost of the Earl of Shrewsbury, with its awe-inspiring polychromed interior: and the much better church of St Augustine, Ramsgate, which he paid for himself.

Other Roman Catholic architects, such as Wardell and Hadfield, produced Puginesque churches: but the Church as a whole was converted to ecclesiology much less completely than the Church of England—as Pugin ruefully acknowledged. Many of the older priests and lay people saw no reason to change their habits; and some of the converts from Anglicanism were anxious to be as Italianate as they could. The Oratorian idea of a large, open church seemed to be common sense: Pugin's dark, mysterious interiors, with screened-off chancels, appeared reactionary.

From the 60s onwards, most of the larger churches were a compromise. The style was Gothic—usually French thirteenth-century, and the plan was orthodox as regards the nave and aisles, but with some un-medieval additions: a row of confessionals projecting from one of the aisles, and an apsidal baptistery somewhere at the west. But the chancel was reduced to one bay, with small chapels at the sides. There was no screen, and, of course, no room for a choir: to put the choir in this position is an Anglican peculiarity. There was usually an apse. The altar made no attempt to be medieval: it had a tabernacle and throne, and an elaborate reredos of white stone with many canopies, pinnacles, and crockets.

Churches like this were designed in large numbers by E. W. Pugin, G. Goldie, and the Hansoms.

J. F. Bentley designed some far more attractive and thoughtful Gothic churches towards the end of the century. The best is the church of the Holy Rood at Watford. Here there is a good-sized chancel, but no screen, though there are rood and rood-loft.

NONCONFORMIST CHURCHES

The eighteenth-century plan lasted on into the second half of the nineteenth century. The Victorian buildings may have a front of debased Renaissance design, but the body remains as before, except that the galleries are usually supported on slender iron columns, and have open ironwork fronts. However, there are some that are still decently Classical.

But Nonconformists were attracted by the Gothic Revival, and soon began to design church-like buildings in First or Second Pointed. Butterfield himself designed Highbury Chapel at Bristol (1842–3) in a quite uncharacteristic Perpendicular style (though he preferred to forget about it). F. J. Jobson, a Methodist, wrote a book called *Chapel and School Architecture*, which is mostly derived from

Pugin. He says that Gothic is Christian architecture, and that it also has the advantage of being the cheapest style.

From about the 60s onward a particular type of Gothic building was erected, in which it must be confessed that far more trouble has been taken over the front than anything else. This is of stone, with a small tower at one side, and a spire surmounted by an ornamental iron finial. On the side opposite to the tower is a projection containing the stairs to the gallery. There is a large window, with two doorways underneath. Behind the front there is nothing in particular. Some architects would design the schoolroom at the back to look, from the outside, like a chancel. But usually there is nothing but the recess for the organ, which, from inside, being filled with the organ, hardly looks like a recess at all.

Free Churchmen are now rather apologetic about this kind of building.

At the turn of the century there was a fashion for a kind of angular Perpendicular, to which even the Baptists succumbed. Examples of such designs may be seen in Crouch and Butler's *Churches, Mission Halls and Schools for Nonconformists* (1901); and the buildings may be seen anywhere. They are generally of bright red brick, with sometimes some terra cotta, and there may be some slightly *art nouveau* details in the ironwork and in the leading of the windows.

(It will be noticed that Crouch and Butler use the word Church in their title: earlier books had referred to Chapels. The word Chapel is not really invidious: it simply means that the building is not the parish church, and it is often used of Roman Catholic places of worship in Ireland. But the word Church has now become almost universal, except in the case of some of the older buildings, such as Wesley's Chapel, City Road.)

THE TWENTIETH CENTURY

In the early part of the twentieth century church building continued along the same lines as in the later nineteenth.

Bodley was still at work. Temple Moore (1856–1920), a pupil of G. G. Scott II, designed a number of beautiful, austere, and refined churches.

Sir J. N. Comper (1866–1960), who had been articled to Bodley, was in the first stage of his career, and was producing restrained and spacious neo-Perpendicular churches, for which he himself designed the glass, the altars, and the woodwork. But he was beginning not to be interested in styles and periods as such, but to aim at 'beauty by inclusion'. A church is good, not because it looks like anything in particular, but only if it 'succeeds in eliminating time and producing the atmosphere of heavenly worship'.

This was the great period of the suburban church. Those who take the trouble to explore the suburbs, and even those who occasionally look out of the window of the train, know that the suburban skyline is broken every mile or two by a large late Victorian or Edwardian church, proud and prosperous-looking (or at least suggesting prosperity in the past, though there is sometimes a feeling that the glory has departed). This was the time when, as someone said, a church had only to be built in the suburbs to be filled at once. It was also a time when building was comparatively cheap. It was usually not too difficult to raise money, and sometimes there was money available from the sale of unwanted churches farther in—which is why so many suburban churches contain unexpected bits of older furnishings. And churchmen and architects were self-confident. So that everything led to the new churches being planned on a large scale.

They are, more often than not, of brick, and have a large nave with narrow aisles and a tall clearstory stage. At the west end is a combination of baptistery and porches. The chancel is raised on flights of steps, and has a chapel on one side: the organ is generally in a loft on the opposite side, and the vestries are spacious.

G. H. Fellowes Prynne (1853–1927) designed many large churches planned like this, often in a rather fantastic kind of Perpendicular.

The churches of W. D. Caröe (1857–1938) are sometimes even more fantastic, with very large west windows, perhaps with buttresses creeping up the mullions, depressed heads, and some very odd tracery.

Unfortunately, very many of these churches have never been completed. When they were begun no one foresaw difficult times ahead, and two-thirds of a church would be built, in the confidence that before long the rest would be completed. But it never was. The stump of the nave remains to this day finished off with a temporary west end of wood. The towers were hardly ever built; and the glass, reredos, and internal decorations were never taken in hand. There is usually an architect's drawing, framed in the vestry, which shows the church as it was meant to be; but the completion was a dream which is never likely to come true.

Bristol is a city that has a large number of such churches, mostly by local architects; but Bristol has been fortunate in its benefactors, and its churches have mostly been finished.

Seaside resorts are always good places for finding large suburban churches. Brighton, St Leonards, and Eastbourne have several: Bournemouth is the best place of all.

The 1914–18 War brought the end of this period and the beginning of the next. Many churches were built in the 20s and 30s, but there were, in general, these differences between them and the earlier ones.

Building became, as it has been becoming ever since, more and more expensive. It was no longer possible to plan very large churches. To build on a big scale to the glory of God is all very well; but if it means a continuous burden of expense for lighting, heating, and repairs, people are less keen about it.

In any case, there has been a growing realization that the Church is a minority in the midst of a pagan world. And that has led to a feeling that a church ought not to be larger than necessary. One church that was built in South London in the 1880s could hold more than the entire population of the parish. No one could want to build that kind of church now.

And at the same time there has come to be a new stress on the corporateness of worship. Corporate is a much overworked word, but the idea is sound enough. The Victorians had it, and they succeeded in realizing it. They said, 'Worship is not simply a duet between the parson and the clerk, to which the people listen in silence.' They taught them to sing the psalms, and they introduced hymns that soon became popular; they removed box pews and galleries, and seated the congregation in open benches, where they could see and be seen. They succeeded in making the Prayer Book services interesting; and they could appeal to the obvious results, if anyone doubted whether their policy had been successful.

But everything is questioned sooner or later, and it was inevitable that, after a time, people should begin to ask, 'Have we, in fact, found the best way of promoting community in worship?' The first question to be raised was about the position of the choir: need it necessarily be in the chancel? And by about 1910 there was nothing very startling in the suggestion that it might be put into a west gallery.

But more recently the matter under discussion has been the position of the altar. Is the east end of the chancel the best place for it? The question does not arise when a new church is being planned, as a chancel is hardly ever included. But ought it even to be in a small recess, such as the pre-ecclesiological churches had? Surely priest and people ought to be brought together as closely as possible, and the people should be made to realize that they are concerned with the liturgy, and have a share in it. Ought not the altar to be in the centre of the building?

Then there is the feeling that a church ought to be contemporary—the opposite point of view to that of Comper, who said that it should be timeless.

'Why', it is asked, 'must they always look back to the past, and imitate something which was natural once, but is natural no longer?' Why indeed? (Except that to the ordinary person association means a great deal, and he is not always at home in a church that seems to have no links with the past. And it is certainly true that buildings that were contemporary a few years ago have a way of looking curiously old-fashioned ten or twenty years after.)

New materials must also have an influence. (Once again, we must be fair to the Victorians, and say that they were aware of this, and were fond of experimenting with the new materials of their age, cast iron and terra cotta.) We have reinforced concrete, and plastics, and new ways of using glass. They must obviously be used: and new ways of construction, and prefabrication, will result in something very different from a medieval Gothic church, or an eighteenth-century building, or a church of the Gothic Revival. New ways of lighting, too, will make a difference to the interior of a church.

Most of the churches that are now being built show some signs of these influences: but the new liturgists and assessors of church designs are, if possible, more dogmatic than the members of the Ecclesiological Society were a century ago, and there are very few new churches that pass their exacting tests.

Nonconformist churches before the 1914-18 War were still usually Gothic. Between the wars, there was a return to simplicity, and an abandonment of the habit of putting the organ in the place of honour.

53

The newest churches are contemporary in style, with lighting of the latest design. There may be a little symbolism in the shape of a plain cross on the end wall, and the Communion table often has flowers.

The general tendency of Roman Catholic churches in this century has been towards Romanesque. Recently, the Liturgical Movement has had its effect on church design and planning, and it can no longer be assumed that a church of the Roman Communion will necessarily be arranged in one particular way, or be filled with objects of piety. A few new churches have been planned for central altars.

The experienced church-hunter, as he approaches one of the older buildings, can almost always tell, without having to look at the notice board, whether it is Church of England, Nonconformist, or Roman Catholic. The most recent churches are far harder to place. This may be a cause for regret: it may seem as though familiar landmarks are being lost, and that the various churches are getting rid of the things that gave them their peculiar character. Or it may seem a hopeful sign—that non-essentials are being scrapped, and that there is a progress towards ultimate reunion. It is too early yet to be sure. But that there has been a general change of outlook in recent years must be obvious to everyone.

PREFACE TO PICTURES

✳ ✳

There are more than 16,000 parish churches in the Church of England and this excludes cathedrals, the chapels of colleges, schools, hospitals, prisons, monasteries and convents as well as chapels-of-ease and mission churches. More than half of these parishes have churches which are nineteenth century and later. This book is an illustrated anthology of these 16,000 parishes in England, which attempts to give a fair proportion of examples of work in every period from the pre-Conquest centuries to the age of modern building estates. If there seem to be too many Victorian churches, that is because there are more Victorian churches than churches of any other age. We have tried to divide Victorian churches into phases in the illustrations.

There is no denying that this book has been compiled from the point of view of the Church of England, to which the Editors belong. But then the medieval parish churches are the charge of the Church and it is greatly to its credit that it has through all the centuries kept them alive and in repair. Much as we may regret the over-enthusiastic 'restoration' done to them by Victorians, let us not forget that without such restoration many of them would have fallen down and that anyhow an equal amount of unsympathetic treatment was given to churches in the last century in most of the countries of Western Europe, particularly France and Belgium. It would have been pleasant to have given fuller illustration of Nonconformist buildings, but we soon realized that these really demand a book to themselves. At a time when so many handsome nineteenth-century Methodist, Baptist and Congregational churches are disappearing from the main streets of English towns and some of the best new churches are Nonconformist, the need for such a book becomes urgent. We have contented ourselves with showing a few of the earlier Nonconformist places of worship (and one late nineteenth-century example) where they fit into the Church of England story. Similarly, too, it would have been pleasant to have shown more Roman Catholic churches and some of the fine buildings put up by the Catholic Apostolic church. Here again we have had to be primarily Anglican because there are so many Anglican churches from which to select. One cannot help noticing how the interiors of many of the late Victorian and Edwardian churches become more Catholic in liturgical arrangement and how in the present day the offsprings of those early Nonconformist churches are beginning to look Anglican inside. Perhaps these are outward and visible signs of a move towards Christian unity.

If this book could have contained all those illustrations I should have wished, more space might have been devoted to the churches on the limestone belt from Lincolnshire to Somerset of the thirteenth and fourteenth centuries and to Devon's fifteenth-century interiors. In the eighteenth century I would have shown more of Hawksmoor and in the nineteenth century more of Butterfield and Bodley and Pearson, and I would have shown some of the work of William White. In the present century a few pages of examples of awful warnings would have served a useful purpose. There are not words fit to express the damage done to old and fine churches by the Electricity Board and some lighting and heating engineers—wires ruthlessly clamped on to old walls from poles, floodlights stuck like surgical basins into medieval roofs, trails of pipes running like railway lines over old walls and meeting at a collection of boxes, metres and switches which is larger and more prominent than any wall monument in the church, electric heaters looking like carpet sweepers fixed on to columns or hanging down from arches, and all in the name of economy and efficiency and none in the name of reverence. It would have been useful, too, to have illustrated examples of the subtopian taste of parochial church councils which tries to turn churchyards into villa gardens with mown lawns and crazy paving and bird baths at the expense of splendid eighteenth-century headstones and gravel paths.

As it is, I would like to thank the knowledgeable Mr Rodney Hubbuck for his enthusiasm in collecting the pictures for the Reverend B. F. L. Clarke and myself, and for ascertaining dates and names and for writing some of the captions.

J. BETJEMAN

PRE-CONQUEST CHURCHES

In Cornwall and the North of England and North Midlands the stone crosses are the earliest relics we have of Christianity after the Romans left Britain. In Cornwall some of them are early sixth century. Sometimes they were set up as gravestones over Christians; sometimes they marked a place where Christianity had been established. Always they were carved, generally with the knots and curly patterns of Celtic decoration such as may be seen in the Book of Kells in the library of Trinity College, Dublin. Where the Celts survived in the north and west of Britain and on the Welsh borders, Celtic carving on fonts and capitals in churches survived until after the Norman Conquest. Stonegrave in Yorkshire (1) is a tenth-century example of Celtic decoration in stone. These stone crosses are usually older than the parish church and show that the Christian faith was taught on the site before the present church was built. These earliest Celtic churches have disappeared from Britain. Some made of unmortared stone survive in Ireland. They were small cells used by monks who were Britain's first missionaries, the earliest being from the Celtic Church in the West, the later being St Augustine's mission from Rome to Kent at the end of the sixth century and beginning of the seventh.

1 STONEGRAVE · YORKSHIRE NORTH RIDING. A 10th-century cross.

2 REPTON · DERBYSHIRE (10th century with 11th-century columns and vaulting). This crypt under the chancel of a cruciform church once held the tombs of Mercian kings and the shrine of St Wystan. Though the crypt is only 15 feet square by 9 feet high it seems large because Saxon architects had a sense of scale.

The system of parishes by which the Church still works in Britain, with a resident priest, is a late Anglo-Saxon invention. Most Saxon churches were of wood like that which survives much restored at Greensted in Essex. Others in wood have disappeared. Where stone was available Saxons built tall churches with narrow proportions and decorated inside with colour, which has disappeared. They were accomplished draughtsmen as may be seen from their manuscripts. Windows were small and high up; walls were thinner than those built by their Norman successors and better constructed on firmer foundations. Churches were usually of a nave and chancel plan and often with a western porch. In eastern England exterior walls were decorated with strips of stone to look like the timber construction Saxons were used to employing, as at St Peter's, Barton-on-Humber, Lincolnshire (**8**).

3 & 4 ESCOMB · CO DURHAM (7th or 8th century). This small Saxon church was built during the times of Bede. The Saxons here, as often elsewhere, used Roman materials, in this case probably from Vinovia; one or two stones have traces of Roman inscriptions. *right* The interior shows the tall narrow proportions characteristic of most Saxon churches. Long and short masonry, a Saxon building technique, is shown in the chancel arch.

5 HEADBOURNE WORTHY · HAMPSHIRE (early 11th century). There is far more evidence left of Anglo-Saxon sculpture than architecture; nearly every county has some relic of a carving, a cross, or a cross shaft. Hampshire has six sculptured roods, three of them large. This one, now sheltered by an early 16th-century annexe, is placed above the Saxon west doorway to remind those who enter of Our Lord's sacrifice and passion, and indeed of the sacramental nature of the Catholic Christian Church. The rood was mutilated in Elizabethan times, when Bishop Horne of Winchester ordered all the crucifixes in his diocese to be destroyed. Only the outline is left of the larger than life-size figures, giving some idea of the former grandeur of the work.

6 WORMINGTON · GLOUCESTERSHIRE (11th century). This little crucifix, about 2 feet high, is interesting for its unusual iconographic treatment in that more than the hand of God is represented.

7 SELHAM · SUSSEX (c1066). During the Saxon-Norman overlap in the last years of the Saxon period and the earliest years of the Norman, sculptors began to carve the capitals of arches as well as crosses and accessory ornaments. The fully Romanesque capitals of the chancel arch at Selham show the level of attainment the Saxon carvers had reached under Norman influence, if not actual guidance, at the time of the Conquest.

8 BARTON-ON-HUMBER·LINCOLNSHIRE,ST PETER (10th century, the top stage 11th century). One of thirty pre-Conquest towers in Lincolnshire. The southern face shows Anglo-Saxon wall-surface decoration in full play. Pilaster strips carry both round- and triangular-headed arches, and the windows have both types of arch. The western 'porticus' is a rare survival. The later parts of the church were built during the 14th and 15th centuries.

9 THORPE-NEXT-HADDISCOE·NORFOLK (11th century). A small Norfolk round tower, one of the 119 in the county. The lower parts are Saxon with little stone windows set in alternating positions into the flintwork, and the very worn blank arcading is just discernible. They were built round because of the scarcity of stone in Norfolk for quoins and dressings. The belfry stage is Norman.

POST-CONQUEST CHURCHES

From the beginning of church building in England, it was the monasteries which set the lead. Most of our older and smaller parish churches started as mission buildings in the Saxon parishes, and their style was determined by whatever particular monastery had charge over them. When England became part of the Duchy of Normandy, as the Channel Islands still are, in 1066, further impetus was given to church building by Benedictine monks of Cluny in France. They believed in building large and magnificent churches. In those parts of England nearest to France, Hampshire and the south-east, their influence is most noticeable in church architecture. The Saxons had more affinity with Christian Germany, and the style of church building in Herefordshire and on the Welsh borders showed few signs of French influence. All over the country, in the eleventh and twelfth centuries, church building went on. The little wooden Saxon churches were pulled down and rebuilt in stone, with thick walls and small windows high up, and often with the rounded east end, called an apse, favoured by the Cluniac monks. Inside, the walls were painted, and, if there was any stained glass in the windows, it was of the transparent mosaic kind, with thick lines of leading and deep blues, reds, and greens, such as may be seen in Chartres, Bourges, and Canterbury. But stained glass was a luxury reserved for the large monastic churches. Window and door openings were round-headed and often carved with zigzag and other ornament in a semi-circle over the arch, particularly over entrance doors and the arches leading into the chancel. The plan of the average small parish church at this time was usually either an oblong nave, with chancel, either square- or round-ended; or nave and central tower with arches under it, leading to the chancel. Cistercian monks, a stricter form of Benedictines than the Cluniacs, eschewed needless ornament and favoured the square east end. Their ways appealed to the innate puritanism in England and it is the square end of English parish churches which makes them differ, in their later stages, from those of Norman France.

11 KIRKBY LONSDALE · WESTMORLAND (*c* 1090–1100). The three-bay fragment of the northern arcade of a Norman church.

10 *left* LASTINGHAM · YORKSHIRE NORTH RIDING (1078–88). The groined and barrel-vaulted early Norman crypt has three parallel aisles, each bay divided off by plain arches springing from heavy capitals on cylindrical columns.

12 *left* FINGEST · BUCKINGHAMSHIRE (early 12th century). This stout, massive tower is wider than the nave of the church beyond it. Its unusually large size may be explained by the possibility that it originally served as the nave, as was the case with some Saxon towers. The double-gabled roof is 17th-century work.

13 QUENINGTON · GLOUCESTERSHIRE (12th century). Norman doorways are to be found almost everywhere in England. The two richly carved early Norman doorways at Quenington, of which this is the northern one, have a carved tympanum or lunette-shaped panel set within the round of the arch.

14 MELBOURNE · DERBYSHIRE (early 12th century). The nave of an exceptionally large Norman parish church which was nearer an abbey. The church, planned with low western towers, was not finished until the 13th century.

15 TEWKESBURY ABBEY · GLOUCESTERSHIRE (founded 1092, the Norman church completed in 1123). These great columns, seven on each side of the nave, 30 feet high, have a girth of 20 feet. A small triforium pinched between the arches and a clerestory squeezed into the vaulting contrast with and emphasize the monumental scale of the arches. The wide vault of 1349–59 springs gracefully from corbelled heads resting on the capitals of the columns.

16 PORCHESTER PRIORY · HAMPSHIRE (founded 1133). The Norman west front. The formerly cruciform church, set in a corner of the huge Roman walled castle campus, was for only fifteen years monastic. The monks then moved to Southwick.

17 DUNSTABLE PRIORY · BEDFORDSHIRE (1150). Though the eastern parts of this once great church are destroyed, there is still monastic grandeur left in the truncated fragment of the nave and aisles. The south aisle shown here was restored in about 1860; the ribbed quadripartite vault is largely a reconstruction.

18 ROMSEY ABBEY · HAMPSHIRE (begun about 1125). The effect of great height is created by the unbroken vertical shafts carried up full height from the bases of the piers to the wall-plates of the barrel roof (Victorian, designed by Benjamin Ferrey), and by the 'blind' outer arches embracing both arcade arches and triforium. Each bay of the nave is different. The arrangement of two Norman arches returning across the east end of the choir is unique. The east windows are geometrical Decorated.

19 BIRKIN · YORKSHIRE WEST RIDING (c 1160). The apse of the east end.

20 KILPECK · HEREFORDSHIRE (*c* 1110, restored and rebuilt *c* 1150–75). Herefordshire had a distinguished school of sculpture of its own during the 12th century; nowhere is it better seen than at Kilpeck, a complete and unaltered Norman church. The sumptuous carving of this Romanesque Celtic south doorway shows strong Saxon influences.

21 STEETLEY CHAPEL · DERBYSHIRE (*c* 1160). A Norman church much restored and partly reconstructed from ruins in 1880–2 by J. L. Pearson. As a model Norman church it is as complete as Adel, Yorkshire West Riding, Heath chapel, Shropshire, and Barfrestone, Kent. Pearson left largely untouched the worn and weathered carved capitals and columns of the deep south doorway.

22 *right* LANGRIDGE · SOMERSET (12th century). This chancel arch is ornamented with zig-zag moulding and a beaded rim. Set in a niche above it is an early representation of the Virgin and Child, carved well before the medieval cults of Our Lady had fully begun.

23 ALNE · YORKSHIRE NORTH RIDING (12th century). The rich and extremely decorative carving of the south doorway at Alne illustrates what had survived the Norman Conquest, for here are Anglo-Saxon characteristics that must be English workmanship.

24 FISHLAKE · YORKSHIRE WEST RIDING (12th century). A detail from one of the finest and richest late Norman doorways in Yorkshire.

25 ELKSTONE · GLOUCESTERSHIRE (*c* 1180). The east window.

26 KEMPLEY · GLOUCESTERSHIRE, OLD CHURCH (mid 12th century). The chancel arch and walls, like the paintings on them, are Norman. Georgian ceiling and monument.

27 BIGHTON · HAMPSHIRE (late Norman). There are many churches in Hampshire and Sussex with transitional Norman work. Here are a pillar piscina of *c* 1190 and a late Norman font of Purbeck marble of a fairly usual type in this region. The corner columns are lost.

28 CLAYTON·SUSSEX. Wall painting of *c* 1160.

29 CHRISTCHURCH PRIORY·HAMPSHIRE (1090–1120). Of the great Norman church, only this richly arcaded and decorated transept turret, the transepts, and most of the nave and aisles survive. It shows how much 'blind' arcading and patterning were used to embellish the greater churches by 1100. The ground-level arcade of interlacing arches extended round the Norman church. The arches are backed by fish-scale patterning, more common in Normandy than in England.

The origins in England of the pointed arch, which admirers of classical architecture in the seventeenth century thought barbarous and called 'Gothic', are discussed on pages 12–14. Throughout the thirteenth and fourteenth centuries, church architecture was still dominated by monasteries. It was in the big abbey and cathedral churches like Canterbury and Durham that experiments in vaulting an oblong space with stone were first made, which resulted in a pointed arch. These experiments with stone roofing were made because wooden roofs caught fire. The eastern end of Canterbury Cathedral, newly rebuilt, had its wooden roof destroyed by fire in 1174. It was the abbeys, too, who employed schools of glass painting. The new form of pointed stone vaulting concentrated the outward and downward pressure of stone roofs on the points from which the arches sprang. This meant that the walls in these places had to be made extra thick with buttresses. Between the buttresses, the walls could be thinner and these gave scope for larger window openings and, eventually, stone tracery for the display of stained glass. Sculptors exercised their skill on mouldings and capitals of columns and arches. The improvement of navigation at sea and up inland rivers caused stone to be used in districts where it had not, hitherto, been available. Until the Black Death in 1348, many villages increased in size and stability. Though the houses of their inhabitants may have been no more than timber-framed tents or mud-walled cabins, the villagers would have thought it a disgrace to have their church built of anything but stone. Sports were held in the churchyard, and the nave of the church, the people's part of the building, was the most weather-proof structure where the villagers could meet. Aisles were added to the nave and larger windows inserted in the walls for the display of stained glass, showing saints and events in the life of Our Lord. Extra altars and chapels to hold them were added either side of the east end.

Most of our old village churches, except for a few in stone districts where skilled masons lived, are not architecture in the sense of the products of the mind of a single artist, but village building added to by each generation—a new aisle here, a new window there, a spire or a tower, and always in the latest style advocated by the monastery connected with the parish. This went on so long as the great abbeys maintained their influence and England was not consciously a separate nation, but an island off the shores of Christendom.

A brief summary of the convenient names for the earlier phases of Gothic is this: *Transitional* (c 1145–c 1190), the change from round-arched Norman to pointed arches starting with stone vaulting; *Early English* (c 1190–c 1245), narrow arches to windows and doors, deep mouldings; *Decorated* (c 1245–c 1360), wider windows with flowing stone tracery, less deep mouldings but more sculpture of leaves and flowers, particularly on capitals.

30 *right* BOXGROVE PRIORY · SUSSEX (c 1210–25). The Early English choir has an arcade arrangement, found elsewhere only in the smaller choir of Portsmouth Cathedral (c 1180), where two pointed arches are held within a round containing arch. The vaulting with ribs enriched with dog-tooth moulding is ornamented with early 16th-century foliage painting.

31 UFFINGTON · BERKSHIRE (*c* 1175–1200). This is an almost complete Early English church, with strongly moulded details. Most of the walls are still covered with pebble-dash. The octagonal central tower once supported a spire which fell down in 1741 and was replaced with the present top stage and battlements.

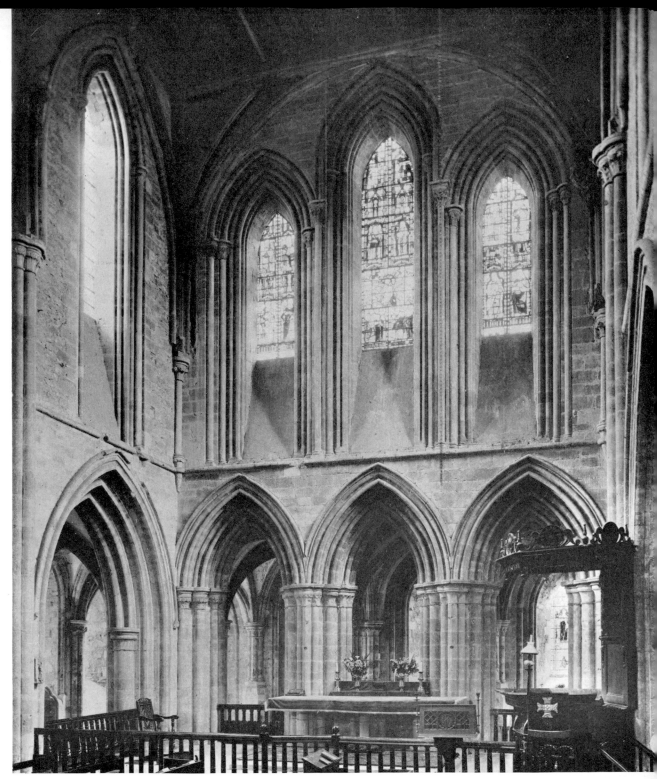

32 ABBEY DORE ABBEY · HEREFORDSHIRE (mid 13th century). The nave, aisles, and conventual buildings of the Cistercian abbey have gone, but there is splendour left in the red sandstone transepts, crossing, presbytery, and aisles, and the two-bay deep ambulatory behind the altar. The church was lovingly restored in 1634 by a local carpenter-architect, John Abel, for Lord Scudamore, who had it made the parish church. John Abel's dark woodwork contrasts happily with the restrained Cistercian architecture, and the lancet windows framed by the delicate mouldings are filled with 17th-century stained glass.

33 ODDINGTON · GLOUCESTERSHIRE (13th century). During the 13th century, many small Norman churches were completely or partially rebuilt, or more often enlarged by an aisle or aisles and the lengthening of the chancel. Sometimes more ambitious work was done. At Oddington, a new church was added on to the old, keeping the Norman building as the south aisle, an unusually conservative way of enlarging a church during the Middle Ages. The pulpit is Jacobean. The Royal arms painted over the chancel arch are Stuart.

34 ASHBOURNE · DERBYSHIRE (*c* 1240). A rich example of the Early English doorway. The colonnettes were renewed in 1840.

35 PERSHORE ABBEY · WORCESTERSHIRE (1223–39). The remains of a Benedictine abbey church, once larger than Worcester Cathedral. The proportions and mouldings equal in quality of workmanship those of the Early English choir at Worcester.

36 MADLEY · HEREFORDSHIRE (13th and 14th centuries). This is an Early English and Decorated interior with walls shorn of their medieval plaster and the sandstone now naked and scraped. But nothing can kill the fine proportions of the interior. Tall, plain cylindrical columns and simply cut arches lead the eye down the long clerestoried nave to the apse, rare in England for the 14th century, with its traceried windows filled with 14th-century stained glass.

37 MINSTER-IN-THANET · KENT (13th century with 12th-century nave and aisles and partly Saxon tower). Stone vaulting as developed by the Normans was continued by the Early English builders, but was rare outside the cathedrals and greater churches. The few village churches with vaulting, almost entirely confined to the chancel, are usually in areas where stone was at hand (north Wiltshire and Gloucestershire) or close to the sea or a wide river on which stone could be shipped and transported. In the Benedictine nunnery church at Minster-in-Thanet, the severe Norman nave contrasts with the graceful Early English vaulted chancel.

38 KIRKSTEAD · LINCOLNSHIRE (13th century). The little gatehouse chapel or 'Capella-extra-Portas' is all that is left, except for a fragment of the transepts of the church, of the buildings of the great Cistercian Abbey of Kirkstead. During the 18th century the chapel was used as a conventicle for the local Presbyterians, and their canopied pulpit is seen in this old photograph.

39 EAST HENDRED · BERKSHIRE (*c* 1200). It is hard to say whether this was a rustic attempt to copy a Roman Corinthian capital or the invention of its carver.

40 PILLERTON HERSEY · WARWICKSHIRE (13th century). The usual Early English east window consisted of three stepped-up narrow pointed windows called 'lancets'. Here is a variation on the triplet of lancets, that in the middle being wider than those which flank it. Above is a quatrefoil window within a circular aperture, the complete ensemble framed within a 'blind' containing arch. The wooden roof is Victorian.

41 BOTTESFORD · LINCOLNSHIRE (13th century). The proportions of this lofty interior, especially the chancel, are on a grand scale, yet this is not an unusually large church for Lincolnshire. The effect of great height is brought about by the large expanses of the walls above the arcades and chancel arch, also by the excessively long and narrow side lancet lights of the deep and lofty chancel. Nothing of the medieval colour or texture is left; the walls are hideously skinned of their medieval plaster and the Victorian furnishings are unworthy.

42 LONG SUTTON · LINCOLNSHIRE (13th century). A lead-covered wooden spire: this is an early one, if not the earliest. The lead sheets are applied diagonally over the timber framework; where there has been patching it is haphazard. With its orb-crowned corner spirelets, this spire rises from an arcaded tower which is detached from the church. Other notable leaden spires include Godalming (Surrey), Barnstaple, Braunton, and Swimbridge (Devon), Hadleigh (Suffolk), East Meon (Hampshire), and Hemel Hempstead (Hertfordshire). The most crooked of them all is Chesterfield.

43 BRIDLINGTON PRIORY · YORKSHIRE EAST RIDING
(late 13th and early 14th centuries). The surviving
lofty nave of the former Augustinian Priory church is
largely an example of the earliest geometrical phase
of the Decorated period. The early 14th century's
fondness for geometrical forms in window tracery
is evident in the north triforium and clerestory.

44 EATON BRAY · BEDFORDSHIRE. A 13th–15th century
church with 13th-century arcades. The Victorians
skinned the plaster from the aisle walls.

45 HOWDEN · YORKSHIRE EAST RIDING (west front finished in the first decade of the 14th century). In the west front of the formerly collegiate Minster church of Howden is seen a Yorkshire type of façade design. As at the east front of Selby Abbey, thick buttresses, proportioned to the façade and west window, support spired octagonal lantern turrets rich with open tracery.

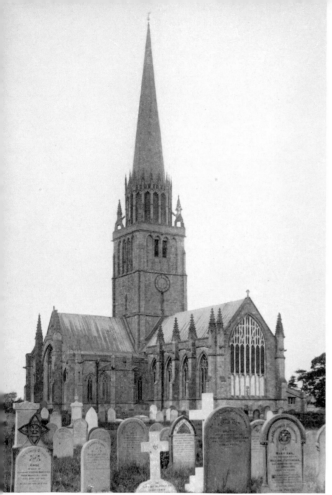

46 PATRINGTON · YORKSHIRE EAST RIDING (14th and 15th centuries). A cruciform church, partly stone-vaulted. It was all designed by one architect in the late 14th century except for the east window which was put in in the early 15th century after the Black Death. Inside and out, it is of a sturdier, thicker Yorkshire type, and has the unusual distinction, shared by only three other medieval English churches, of double transept aisles. But the chief glory of Patrington is the crossing tower and spire, the latter with its coronet. The little triagonal apsed Lady chapel is unique.

47 BEVERLEY MINSTER · YORKSHIRE EAST RIDING (begun *c* 1225 with the east end, the church completed with the west front and towers in *c* 1420). In this great pilgrimage church is shown a continuous logical evolution of the styles of three periods, each harmonising with the others. A restrained nave leads to the elaborate choir with its stalls with misericords, the Percy tomb, and the altar screen.

48 MUNSLOW · SHROPSHIRE (early 14th century). An unusual variety of early Decorated window tracery. The leaded clear glass is late Georgian.

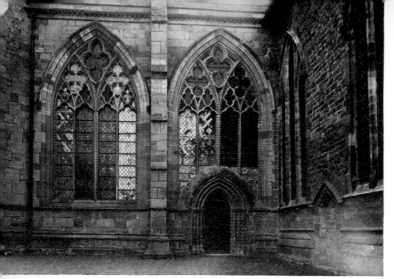

49 LEDBURY · HEREFORDSHIRE (14th century). The west windows of St Catherine's chapel, the north transept of this large, mostly 14th-century church, are enriched with ball-flower ornament. This decorative motif, which mostly appears on windows and doorways, replaced the 13th-century dog-tooth ornament. Ball flower is a misnomer, for it may have derived from the opening bud of the apple blossom. It was introduced earlier and persisted longer in the orchard counties of Hereford and Worcester.

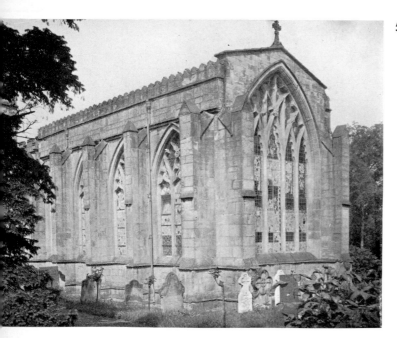

50 NORBURY · DERBYSHIRE (c 1355–70). During the 14th century in Derbyshire a number of unusually large, fine chancels were built that were almost as long as the naves of the churches. Norbury, with its rich window tracery, and internal spaciousness, is one of this Derbyshire group of Decorated churches which includes Chaddesden, Dronfield, Sandiacre, and Tideswell.

51 NAVENBY · LINCOLNSHIRE (14th century). Decorated window tracery in the chancel.

52 *right* FLEET · LINCOLNSHIRE (14th century). This tower is detached from the rest of the church.

53 TYDD ST MARY·LINCOLNSHIRE (mainly 14th century, with a 15th-century tower of brick with stone dressings and spire). This early photograph (1859) shows what Lincolnshire churches looked like before the Victorians raised the pitch of the roofs and scraped the texture off the walls.

54 HIGHAM FERRERS · NORTHAMPTONSHIRE (14th century). The large, but not identical, twin east windows of this mainly Decorated Nene-valley church are filled with reticulated 14th-century tracery. Their ogeed tops support canopied niches.

55 DORCHESTER ABBEY · OXFORDSHIRE (largely 14th century, but with earlier and later work). Formerly an Augustinian abbey church.

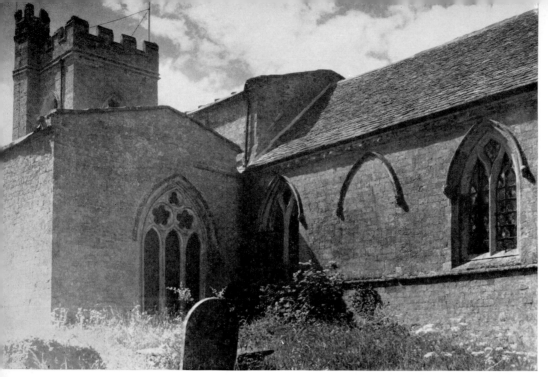

56 HANWELL · OXFORDSHIRE (14th-century chancel and south aisle). The church is built of the same orange stone as the village.

57 HAWTON · NOTTINGHAMSHIRE (c 1330). The north chancel doorway and founder's canopied tomb-recess group with the Easter Sepulchre. This was always placed on the north side of the chancel (usually in the sanctuary), and held the Blessed Sacrament from Good Friday until Easter Day. The carving represents the Resurrection and Ascension of Christ.

58 WOLFHAMCOTE · WARWICKSHIRE (14th century). Decorated column and capital, medieval and 17th-century woodwork.

59 TROTTON · SUSSEX (late 14th century). Mural paintings were the chief visual aids of the Middle Ages. The illiterate were taught their faith from Bible stories on the walls of churches, and Christian ideas of good and evil values and behaviour were preached in morality or warning paintings. At Trotton, the seven deadly sins are represented coming out of the Evil Man on the left side of the west wall. In the centre Moses upholds the tables of the law beneath Christ in judgement; on the right side are the seven acts of mercy depicted in roundels around the Good Man. The contrast is clear, and with the strong pattern of the roundels emphasis is placed on the right or good side. There are two consecration crosses, one of them seen in this photograph at the feet of the Good Man.

60 EDINGTON PRIORY · WILTSHIRE (1352–61). Was built in nine years by Bishop William of Edington for the Augustinian order of Bonhommes. The church shows the almost imperceptible transition from late Decorated to early Perpendicular. Major developments in the Middle Ages were the result of many years of constant experiment; the evolution of a style took time.

61 CHRISTCHURCH PRIORY · HAMPSHIRE (shortly before the Black Death of 1349). This richly niched and tabernacled stone reredos is behind the high altar.

62 SHOTTESBROOKE · BERKSHIRE (late 14th-century brass of vested priest and layman). The 14th and 15th centuries were the golden age of the monumental brass. The earliest brass in England, at Stoke d'Abernon (Surrey), dates from 1277. From then on the monumental-brass artists flourished. Their industry declined at the Reformation, but began to revive in the first quarter of the 17th century. Despite countless numbers of brasses that were ripped from the matrices during the 16th century and later (the destruction continued, decreasingly, well into the 19th century), several hundreds of them survive, many of them mutilated. The thing to look for in brasses is good drawing. The brass demands a clean, incisive line. Rich canopies, pinnacles, and frames with inscriptions sometimes surround the figures.

63 HAMSTALL RIDWARE · STAFFORDSHIRE (mainly 14th and 15th centuries).
A simple Midlands church with 15th-century clerestory and west windows
and Victorian porch. Inside are old woodwork, screens, tombs, and stained
glass. To the north stand the remains of the manor house.

64 BLISLAND · CORNWALL. A rood and painted screen restored by F. C. Eden early in this century to a village church largely rebuilt in the 15th century.

ENGLISH PERPENDICULAR
(c 1360–c 1485)

There is hardly a medieval parish church in England without traces of work of this period and most churches were greatly enlarged at this time. The word 'Perpendicular' aptly describes the style, for it is characterized by long, thin vertical lines of stone and tracery in the windows, greater areas of glass, taller and thinner columns for arcades, and tall towers. Inside the churches was a greater effect of height, space, and light. This, combined with stained-glass windows, walls painted with legends of saints, the Last Judgement, painted wooden screens, shrines, and altars, produced a splendour not seen in parish churches before.

Abbeys were emptying and declining in influence. Mendicant friars, Augustinian and Dominican, had started popular preaching so that in the fifteenth century there was a medieval foretaste of the Methodist revival of the eighteenth century. Special churches were built for the friars. Naves of parish churches were extended to hear them preach, and pulpits and carved wooden benches were put in the nave.

The important men of England were no longer abbots and barons. Landowners and wealthy wool merchants added chapels to the east of the church or rebuilt the chancel and hired priests to say Mass for themselves, their family, and forbears, and commemorated themselves in brasses, stained glass, and stone effigies. In the towns trade guilds built chapels on to the parish churches and hired priests and paid to keep lights burning on the altars. The cult of Our Lady, who was deeply beloved by the English, flourished and chapels were added to churches in her honour. Our Lord was thought of very much as God become Man and the Son of Our Lady, and His Figure hanging on the Cross above the chancel screen dominated the nave of the church which was strewn with rushes and sweet-smelling herbs and where plays were acted. In the porch of the church the first schools started. In the churchyard were no headstones because the common people were buried in wool not very deep and were commemorated inside the church in the prayers of chantry priests while sports were held and ale was handed out on the grass of the churchyard outside. Birth and death were near and unhygienic.

'The pious English' was the phrase used about our country by foreigners. Though the origins of the Perpendicular style came from the court of France and it was first seen at the beginning of the fourteenth century in London in the friars' churches and St Stephen's Chapel, Westminster, it developed in the prosperous fifteenth century into a native English style with regional characteristics, and marked off England as becoming a consciously separate country from the continent. It was the people's style and that is why it is primarily associated with the nave, the people's part of the church, and chantry chapels of families and trade guilds and big town churches.

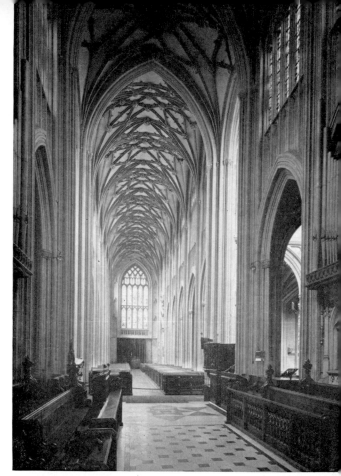

65 BRISTOL · ST MARY, REDCLIFFE (mainly 15th century, but with earlier parts from *c* 1180 onwards). Perpendicular height—a testament to the civic and merchant wealth of the second city and port of medieval England. The church may have been planned on the cathedral scale so as to eclipse in splendour the churches of the rival city of London.

66 ASTBURY · CHESHIRE (mostly 15th century). Perpendicular breadth. Perpendicular style.

67 MALPAS · CHESHIRE. Mainly late 15th century with a 14th-century tower. The upper room of the two-storied south porch may have been used for a variety of purposes, as a priest's room, schoolroom, parish library, or even as a store for armour. The pink sandstone of Cheshire churches weathers badly and has been much renewed by Victorians.

68 LAUNCESTON · CORNWALL, ST MARY MAGDALENE (1511–24). One of the final flings of Cornish Perpendicular, it was built by Sir Henry Trecarrel. This large town church, of three parallel aisles 103 feet long, was erected on the site of an earlier chapel, of which the late 14th-century tower was kept. The whole granite exterior is profusely decorated with panelled ornament. The intricate floral and heraldic motifs are of painstaking workmanship since the very hard rough material does not allow precision.

69 ST BLAZEY · CORNWALL (15th century). Built of large granite blocks held together with grey cement mortar-courses. The windows are of the standard Cornish production with simple characteristic tracery and thick hood moulds. Most Cornish churches were rebuilt in the 15th century.

70 WINTERBOURNE ST MARTIN · DORSET (late 15th century). An unassuming church. Most of the windows of the church, set in mossy yellow-ochre roughcast walls, are square-headed and must be of later date.

71 BEAMINSTER · DORSET (early 16th century).

72 GATCOMBE · ISLE OF WIGHT (late 15th century). The prevailing style of Isle of Wight churches is 15th century, closer to Dorset than to Hampshire in type. Building stone on the island is varied, and the variety of stones is shown from one village to the next in the different colours.

73 CREWKERNE · SOMERSET (mostly late 15th and early 16th centuries). The west front.

74 WRINGTON · SOMERSET (1420–50). The bell-chamber windows continue down to the stage below to emphasize verticality, a Somerset device. To the limestone belt of England from Lincolnshire through Rutland, Northamptonshire, and the Cotswolds to Somerset, the wool trade brought prosperity in the 15th and 16th centuries. Villages rivalled one another in splendour of towers, particularly in Somerset.

75 IPPLEPEN · DEVON (mainly 15th century). From the top down, the three stages are bell chamber, ringing chamber, and west window to light the nave. In Devon the arrangement of angle buttresses and newel-stair turret are turned into features to emphasize the vertical lines while horizontal bands of stone (string courses) emphasize proportion.

76 *right* ISLE ABBOTS · SOMERSET. The tower is *c* 1500. Pierced stone louvres to let out the sound of the bells; saints in the niches.

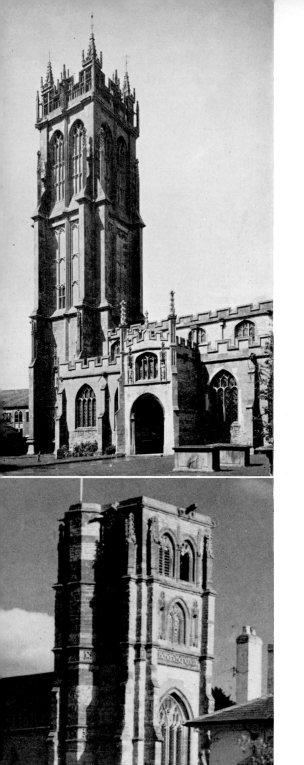

77 *above left* GLASTONBURY · SOMERSET, ST JOHN (1460–90). Built by Abbot John Selwood, this is the second highest of the Somerset church towers.

78 *above* BATCOMBE · SOMERSET (c 1540). Set in a canopied niche over the apex of the west window of the tower is a figure of Christ standing on a globe. On the wall around are angels, the two upper ones censing, the lower ones with emblems of the Passion.

79 RUISHTON · SOMERSET (c 1530–5). Many Somerset church towers were not completed until well into the 16th century. This little tower was never finished; building was halted at the Reformation.

80 STEEPLE ASHTON · WILTSHIRE (1480–1500)
The fan-vaulted south aisle, designed by Thomas
Lovell and built by Walter Lucas and his wife.

81 CIRENCESTER · GLOUCESTERSHIRE (15th and
16th centuries). The largest of all Cotswold
'wool' churches, built by rich wool merchants.
The tower is panelled like several other towers
in Gloucestershire.

82 WINCHCOMBE · GLOUCESTERSHIRE (begun *c* 1460). This complete 'wool' church of the Cotswolds was built all at the same time.

83 BLEDINGTON · GLOUCESTERSHIRE (15th century). The strainer arch marks off the chantry chapel from the chancel. Where the bell stands was an altar for a chantry priest to say Mass. A screen under the arch must once have divided this little chapel from the chancel of the church from which this photograph was taken.

84 LUTON · BEDFORDSHIRE (externally, largely 15th century). The tower, aisles, transept chapels and east end were added to the town church in about 1461 and are distinguished by their chequerboard walls of stone and flint.

85 BRIDLINGTON PRIORY · YORKSHIRE EAST RIDING (c 1480). The west front has one of the largest windows in Yorkshire, similar to the east window at Beverley. (See also **43**.)

86 & 87

BEVERLEY · YORKSHIRE EAST RIDING, ST MARY (1520–4). In Yorkshire there is a definite local type of tower. Unlike the towers of Somerset, towers cannot be classified into groups. St Mary, Beverley, has one of the finest, a sturdy crossing tower with panelled battlements and a forest of crowning pinnacles. The circular windows in the lower stage are unusual. Other fine 15th-century Yorkshire towers are at Cottingham, Hatfield, Hedon, and Tickhill. Streets and alleys in medieval towns and villages, as shown here, generally are so sited as to show two sides of the tower at once so as to give a look of solidity. *below* The nave and tower of the church were rebuilt after the fall of the old 12th-century tower in 1520.

88 BURWELL · CAMBRIDGESHIRE (mostly mid 15th century, the nave roofed in 1464, with earlier parts). In East Anglia, when they added aisles with large windows, they raised the nave roof and lit it with clerestory windows to show the woodwork within.

89 WALPOLE ST PETER · NORFOLK (*c* 1390–1410). This is the finest church of the Marshes. The absence of any severe restoration work is evident inside and out.

90 *left* SALLE · NORFOLK (first half of 15th century). It stands alone in the fields and was raised by the families who owned the land and was built entirely at one time. The windows have mostly lost their medieval stained glass.

91 *left* KING'S LYNN · NORFOLK, ST NICHOLAS (beginning of 15th century, the old Early English tower has been retained). This vast chapel-of-ease to St Margaret's is of an overwhelming size even for East Anglia. Its great breadth shows the influence of friars who liked large broad naves in which to preach to the people.

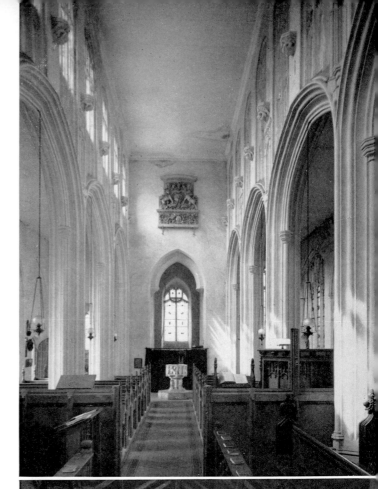

92 SHELTON · NORFOLK (*c* 1487). The poppy-headed pews and arcades and font are 15th century. The ceiling and Royal arms are Georgian.

93 SOUTH CREAKE · NORFOLK (predominantly 15th century but with earlier chancel and other parts). The ideal Norfolk interior: wide, light, with white plastered walls and clear spaces, brick-paved and partly stone-flagged floors, medieval screen, wooden pulpit, a clerestory, and medieval roofs, nave and aisles.

96 *right* FRAMLINGHAM · SUFFOLK (late 15th century). The tower, built of flint interspersed with random blocks of white stones, sparkles in strong sunlight. It is 96 feet high and powerfully built, with a flushwork panelled base and plainer panelled angle buttresses.

94 STOKE-BY-NAYLAND · SUFFOLK (15th century). The tower was built of brick by local merchants. Diagonal buttresses are panelled with canopied niches and the windows are deeply recessed.

95 SYLEHAM · SUFFOLK (largely 15th century). A small Suffolk church with one of the 41 Suffolk round towers. The south porch may have been built by Alice de la Pole, Duchess of Suffolk: it bears the arms of her parents and her husband.

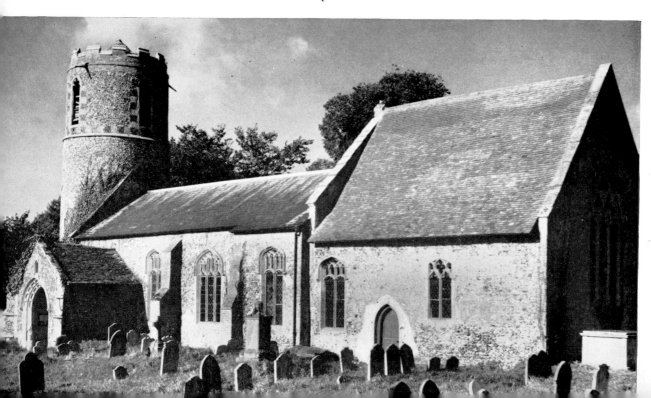

97 BLYTHBURGH · SUFFOLK (15th century, with earlier tower). Once Blythburgh was a thriving port and town; now only a few cottages and the great church, shorn of much of its medieval glory, remain.

98 EYE · SUFFOLK (1460–80). Vertical panels of flint and stone known as 'flushwork' decorate and emphasize the proportions of the tower.

99 DENSTON · SUFFOLK (shortly before 1475). A chantry college of priests was founded here by Sir John Howard and John Broughton after the church had been rebuilt. The east window is a kaleidoscope of fragments of medieval glass which has escaped the iconoclasm of William Dowsing, the 17th-century puritan who went round East Anglia smashing glass and carving. The high Jacobean pulpit and the old pews survive. The church was considerately restored by Martin Travers in the 1930s.

100 THAXTED · ESSEX (14th, 15th, and early 16th centuries). A church of gradual but consistent growth reflecting the prosperity of the affluent late medieval town. The Decorated arcades, leading into aisles wider than the high narrow nave, are crowned by clerestory windows of *c* 1510 with panelled splays. The church was restored by Randall Wells in about 1920.

101 COVENTRY · WARWICKSHIRE, HOLY TRINITY (15th-century clerestory and roof). The spandrels of the cross ribs carry angels with shields bearing the instruments of the Passion. The panels are studded with stars.

102 WARWICK · WARWICKSHIRE, ST MARY: THE BEAUCHAMP CHAPEL (1443–62). The lavishly panelled exterior is unusual and rich with its outer pinnacles connected by open tracery. The chapel contains the magnificent tomb of Warwick the Kingmaker. (See **113**.)

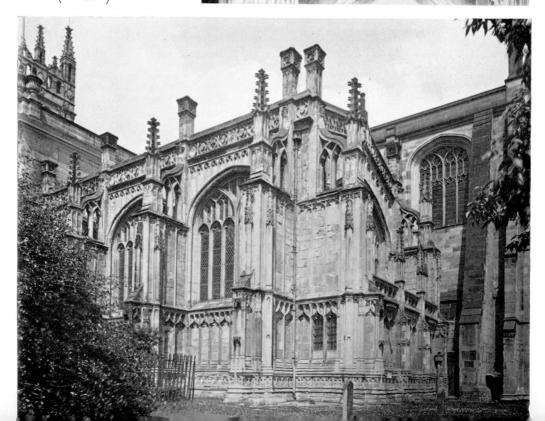

103 SHERBORNE ABBEY · DORSET (south choir aisle of the first half of 15th century). Sherborne Abbey is largely a Perpendicular recasting of a late Norman fabric. Most of the arches throughout the church are panelled in a style which spread to many Somerset and Dorset churches.

104 CIRENCESTER · GLOUCESTERSHIRE (*c* 1500). The passageway beneath the south porch with its fan-vaulted ceiling. The upper chambers of the porch served as the town hall. (See **81**.)

106 DARTMOUTH · DEVON, ST SAVIOUR (15th century).
Cornish and Devon men were boat-builders and
carpenters. They loved carving, and executed benchends, screens, and pulpits. This pulpit is one of the
ten stone pulpits in Devon.

107 TALLAND · CORNWALL (c 1537–47). Carved benchends
are to be found in profusion in the West Country. At
Talland there is a fine set of the usual Cornish standard
type of design. This Tudor example has Renaissance
heads in the panels. There are benchends of a very
different type in Norfolk and Suffolk, where the carving
is mostly on poppyheads.

105 *left* STOKE-BY-NAYLAND · SUFFOLK (south door
15th century). Many Perpendicular doors were decorated with tracery, but very seldom were they as rich
as the south door at Stoke-by-Nayland, where figures
in canopied niches illustrate the Tree of Jesse. The oak has
turned silvery-grey with age.

108 RANWORTH · NORFOLK (15th century). Norfolk is rich in surviving rood screens; Ranworth has one of the best of them, complete with its side altars and painting. The panels of rood screens were usually painted with figures of saints.

109 EWELME · OXFORDSHIRE (late 15th century). The font was sometimes given a spired and tabernacled canopy which could be raised by pulley; sometimes the canopy would stand on columns, as at St Peter Mancroft, Norwich, and Trunch. Here canopied arches taper into a crocketed pinnacle crowned by the winged figure of St Michael the Archangel. The canopy was carefully restored in 1832.

110 DENNINGTON · SUFFOLK (15th century). Parclose screens fill the arches between chancel and chapels or shut off the easternmost bays of nave aisles into chantry chapels. This detail of the screenwork to the Bardolf chantry chapel at Dennington shows the mullions and tracery painted with delicate patterns.

111 CHURCH HANBOROUGH · OXFORDSHIRE (15th century). A side chapel screen which is an extension of that of the chancel. The front of the projecting loft is decorated with carved trailing vines.

112 KINLET · SHROPSHIRE (15th century). A detail of one of the mourners of the alabaster tomb
to Sir Humphrey Blount, d. 1477, and wife. Little figures of mourners or 'weepers' were
often placed under arches or canopies in the sides of tombs; they sometimes held shields with
coats of arms.

113 WARWICK · WARWICKSHIRE, ST MARY (15th century). The monument to Richard Beauchamp, Earl of Warwick, was made in 1447–53, to designs by John Essex. Most 15th-century tombs were of this type, but few were as grand.

114 HESSETT · SUFFOLK (15th century). This detail of the south porch shows knapped flints with a random sprinkling of stones; the panelled base has apparently lost the flint flushwork which filled the panels.

115 TEWKESBURY ABBEY · GLOUCESTERSHIRE: TOMB OF ABBOT WAKEMAN (early 16th century). The gruesome sculpture of the corpse is in contrast to the delicate carved stone-work above and beneath it.

116 OTHERY · SOMERSET (15th-century cope). Several churches have relics of medieval needle-work, especially copes and altar frontals. This velvet cope is embroidered with silver threads.

117 COMBE · OXFORDSHIRE (15th century). Mural painting of the Crucifixion.

118 BEETHAM · WESTMORLAND (late 15th or early 16th century). The 15th century was a great period for English stained glass; schools of glass painting flourished at Norwich and York. Very few complete windows survive; York is the best place to find them. More or less complete sets of windows survive at Fairford, Gloucestershire, and St Neot, Cornwall. The ground of this Crucifixion panel is patterned with tear-drop shapes that symbolize drops of Christ's blood.

119 COLN ROGERS · GLOUCESTERSHIRE (15th century). St Margaret. Most ancient stained glass is fragmentary, and often confined to small tracery lights overlooked by iconoclasts.

120 YARNTON · OXFORDSHIRE (15th century). This angel wears the feathered finery of a peacock, and is set in an oval medallion composed of fragments from destroyed stained-glass windows.

121 RADDINGTON · SOMERSET (largely 15th century). Prosperity and Perpendicular splendour were not everywhere. Some churches remained the nave-and-chancel buildings they were when they were first built in permanent material. They are village buildings, altered now and then to let in more light or to add a single aisle. This church in the hills near Exmoor has no lane leading to it. The floor of the porch is cobbled; the wooden doorway and door have medieval iron hinges.

122 AMPNEY ST MARY · GLOUCESTERSHIRE (12th century, with work of the 13th, 14th, and 15th centuries). This little church is a compendium of work from nearly all periods of medieval architecture. During the 13th century the Norman chancel was lengthened.

123 STOCK · ESSEX (15th century). In poorer districts, or where stone was scarce and timber plentiful, churches were constructed of wood. Shropshire and Cheshire have many 'black-and-white' timber churches. In the home counties and Hampshire, timber is often used for belfries and porches. South Essex is noted for its timber belfries, which take on shapes and arrangements not found elsewhere. At Stock there is an ambulatory ground floor, over which rises a weatherboarded belfry and shingled spire. Other belfries of weatherboarded timber of particular interest are at Blackmore and West Hanningfield.

124 PENHURST · SUSSEX (15th century). Timber porches are so common in the home counties that they are almost an expected feature of an old church. At Penhurst the wood has weathered silvery-grey, the grain furrowed and worn deep by the elements. Lichen mottles the bricks, tiles, and weathered wealden stones.

The Perpendicular style did not die out suddenly. It lingered on in church building through the sixteenth century and even into the reign of James I. Arches were flatter and sometimes windows were square-headed. The classical architecture of the Renaissance in Italy mostly came to this country second-hand from prints in books printed in the Low Countries. Attempts at a classical style are found in the carving of woodwork and stone monuments. The internal arrangement of sixteenth-century churches was the same as before the Reformation—chancel, nave and aisles. Screens were retained or new built, but the figure of Our Lord crucified was taken down from over the top of them and the Royal arms substituted. The Tudors thought of the monarch as Defender of the Faith as well as head of the state.

125 ST OSYTH · ESSEX (early 16th century). Brick was used to a considerable extent in Essex from the late 15th century. There are about thirty brick towers, and several brick porches and chapels, some added late in the 16th century and early in the following century. Tudor brick arcades such as these are rare in England.

126 BARTON-UNDER-NEEDWOOD · STAFFORDSHIRE (1533). A rare, wholly early 16th-century village church built when the monasteries were on the verge of dissolution, and when the Renaissance was gaining hold. This church is still conventional 15th century in plan and form; only the windows are recognisably Tudor, and there is no suggestion of Renaissance influence.

127 BOXGROVE PRIORY · SUSSEX: DE LA WARR CHANTRY (1532). Tudor Gothic and Renaissance details are mixed in the design of this chantry chapel erected shortly before the dissolution of the Priory. The vaulting is a hanging canopy of lace-like flamboyant tracery in strong white stone. This is typical of the mentality of the age which arranged the Field of the Cloth of Gold.

128 SEFTON · LANCASHIRE (c 1535–40). The further north, the more conservative: Sefton, one of the great churches of the north-west, reflects entirely the larger Cheshire churches of the 15th century; there is not even a 'debased' or square-headed window. The church is fitted with screen, loft, and stalls. This is a detail of the eastern side of the screen.

129   SUNNINGWELL · BERKSHIRE (*c* 1562). A detail of the unique seven-sided porch built by Bishop Jewel, probably the work of Oxford masons. Here the full effect of the Renaissance is shown, but still there are Tudor Gothic windows. The Elizabethan period was until recently thought to have been one of almost complete inactivity in church building, repair, and restoration, but recent research has discovered about 150 examples of it.

130   LANGLEY CHAPEL · SHROPSHIRE (1601, or perhaps 1564). This simple country chapel has its complete complement of Jacobean furnishings untouched by later work.

131 LEEDS · YORKSHIRE WEST RIDING, ST JOHN (1632–4). This is a Gothic Survival church of twin-nave plan. The Carolean furnishing was very nearly lost in the 1860s, but it was saved, and well restored by young Norman Shaw.

132 CROSCOMBE · SOMERSET. Jacobean furnishings (1616).

133 FRAMLINGHAM · SUFFOLK : MONUMENT TO THOMAS HOWARD THIRD DUKE OF NORFOLK (1554). In about 1554 the chancel at Framlingham was rebuilt on a grand scale to house the magnificent Howard Monuments. This is one of the finest mid 16th-century Renaissance monuments in England.

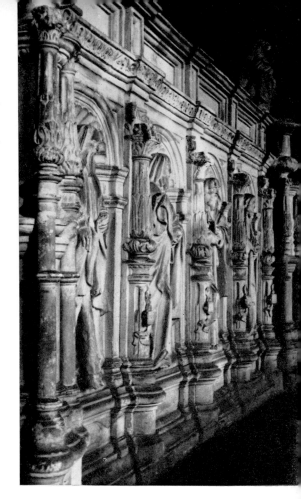

134 *below left* STRENSHAM · WORCESTERSHIRE : MONUMENT TO THOMAS RUSSELL (1618). The recumbent figures with a lion at their feet are still medieval in treatment and pose. The rest of the monument is Renaissance.

135 *below right* OXFORD · ST MARY THE VIRGIN : THE SOUTH PORCH (1637). This porch, with its twisting columns, and its scroll-covered broken pediment and central niche with a statue of the Virgin and Child, gets as near to the Baroque style as anything in 17th-century England, except for monuments.

136 GUYHIRN · CAMBRIDGESHIRE, OLD CHURCH (1660). Puritan austerity is illustrated by this long plain whitewashed room furnished with holy table, pulpit, and open pews. Here men could concentrate on prayer without the distractions of art.

137 BROUGHAM (NINEKIRKS) · WESTMORLAND (1660). This humble little church is just as it was when the remarkable Lady Anne Clifford (1590–1676) rebuilt it. Lady Anne restored the two churches at Appleby, churches at Bardon, Bongate, Mallerstang, Skipton (1655), and the nearby St Wilfrid, Brougham.

MEDIEVAL CHURCHES ADAPTED TO PRAYER-BOOK WORSHIP

Despite the infiltration of extreme protestant doctrines in the sixteenth and seventeenth centuries, the English Church retained the catholic creeds and the two sacraments essential to salvation—Baptism and Holy Communion. The other five sacraments were also retained but not insisted on. The chief objects of the more moderate reformers were to make the services more audible and comprehensible to the common people and to encourage congregations to receive the Sacrament at Holy Communion instead of letting the priest do it for them, as had been the custom in the late Middle Ages. The long daily offices of monks were condensed into Matins and Evensong, and the naves of churches were adapted for this purpose. The priest usually read the office from a desk below the pulpit and below him was often a second desk for 'the clerk', a survival from the server at the altar, to make the responses. As sermons were long and Matins, Ante-Communion, Litany, and Evensong long enough, and the whole congregation was expected to attend, pews were arranged round the pulpit and its desks. Pews were given doors and sometimes high partitions to exclude draughts in these now old, cold buildings. Paintings on the walls were whitewashed over and scripture texts painted in their place. Colour was introduced on monuments and in hatchments displaying the arms of deceased members of big families; stained glass did not die out and transparent pictures painted on glass with enamel were an art of the late eighteenth century.

The chancel was used for Holy Communion and rails were erected round the altar that people might kneel to receive the Sacrament. Around the font near the entrance to the church were pews for godparents and parents at baptisms. In every county one or two examples survive of medieval churches thus adapted to prayer-book worship. Most however were scraped and rearranged by the Victorians.

138 WHITBY·YORKSHIRE NORTH RIDING (partly mid 12th-century church remodelled internally in the 18th century, with 18th-century fittings). Galleries painted white surround the dark shapes of the high pulpit and lectern. Over all a flat boarded roof with a skylight recalls the lower decks of old ships. The stovepipe, so often the hallmark of an unrestored interior, completes the picture.

139 PUDDLETOWN · DORSET: LAUDIAN FITTINGS (1635) IN AN INTERIOR OF ABOUT 1500.
The reign of William Laud as Archbishop of Canterbury was a time of considerable rearrangement of the furnishings of churches. There is a west gallery for the choir. This photograph was taken in 1906 before a few minor alterations and the removal of the Gothic
organ.

140 BRADWELL-JUXTA-COGGESHALL · ESSEX (church is mostly 12th century, 18th-century fittings, and 15th-century screen). There are a boarded tympanum and extensive traces of medieval wall-paintings. Many small church interiors looked like this one in 1800 before the onslaught of Victorian restoration.

141 HOLCOMBE · SOMERSET (12th-century church, refashioned in the 16th century and later, early 17th-century pulpit, and early 19th-century hat-pegs). Three-decker pulpit for sermon, offices, and clerk.

142 WINTERBORNE TOMSON · DORSET (12th-century church, early 18th-century south windows, 18th-century fittings). This, one of the four single-cell apsidal Norman churches in England, is completely unrestored. The pews are all Georgian.

143 FAIRFIELD · KENT (15th century, possibly earlier). Fairfield, completely restored in 1913 by W. D. Caröe, has a lovely timber-framed interior with white painted box pews and three-decker pulpit.

144 ABBOTSBURY · DORSET (largely rebuilt *c* 1500). The arcades are late 15th century and similar to those at Puddletown. The plastered barrel ceiling of the chancel is dated 1638. The Jacobean pulpit with its tester and panelled backboard is one of the finest of several in this area. The Classical reredos with a pediment crowned with urns frames the decalogue. The pews are Victorian.

145 WASING · BERKSHIRE (1761 and 1826). A Georgian remodelling of a humble 15th-century church. Some other churches like this are at Chalbury (Dorset), Farley Chamberlayne (Hampshire), and Wheatfield (Oxfordshire).

146 WIDFORD · OXFORDSHIRE (18th-century box pews in a mostly 14th-century church). Unrestored churches are rare; there may be about an average of four per county.

147 WARHAM ST MARY · NORFOLK (15th century). A Georgian three-decker pulpit.

NONCONFORMITY

To some of those who protested against Rome, the Church of England, by maintaining the sacraments and bishops and priests, was unscriptural. During the Commonwealth these extreme protestants had full liberty and some occupied the livings of Anglicans who had been ejected as too High Church under Cromwell. After the Restoration in 1660 extreme protestants were persecuted for a short time, then allowed liberty of worship. The first English Nonconformist chapels were built late in the seventeenth century and belong to Presbyterians, Unitarians, Independents (Congregationalists), Baptists (General and Particular), and Quakers. The meeting houses of the last are very simple buildings with open benches only. The rest are chiefly designed as preaching houses with seats and galleries towards the pulpit. Below the pulpit there was sometimes a table for the celebration of the Lord's Supper. Baptists used ponds and streams for the total immersion of believers. The earliest buildings are simple and cottage-like outside, with clear windows; they are plain and whitewashed within and sometimes, particularly in Unitarian churches, with carved joinery. The Methodists under John Wesley built separate preaching houses from the middle of the eighteenth century onwards. In some parts of England their members attended the parish church at Christmas, Easter, and Whitsun to receive Holy Communion. By the end of the nineteenth century this custom had almost died out and Methodists had their own Communion services. The later Georgian Nonconformist chapels are nearly always classical buildings with handsome façades on the street.

148 WINSLOW · BUCKINGHAMSHIRE, PARTICULAR BAPTIST CHAPEL (1695). The interiors of most early meeting houses are cottage-like plastered rooms lit by domestic windows filled with latticed or rectangular panes of clear glass, and furnished simply with plain open benches, a Communion table, and a prominent pulpit.

149 WALPOLE·SUFFOLK, CONGREGATIONAL CHAPEL (1647). This interior was created by gutting a dwelling house built in 1607. The earliest Congregational churches, like those of the Baptists, were humble and domestic in character. Walpole was enlarged later in the 17th century, and altered in the following century. The two-decker pulpit has command of galleries on three sides.

150 NORWICH · NORFOLK, THE OCTAGON CHAPEL, COLEGATE (1754–6). This octagonal preaching house by the Norwich architect, Thomas Ivory, was originally built for Presbyterians and is now Unitarian.

151 BRISTOL · GLOUCESTERSHIRE, WESLEY'S CHAPEL—'WESLEY'S NEW ROOM' (1739, enlarged 1748). The earliest of all Wesleyan Methodist churches, founded by John Wesley himself. In this galleried interior are seen the characteristic early Wesleyan liturgical arrangements that were the rule in nearly all Methodist churches until about 1900. The chapel was well restored in this century by Sir George Oatley.

152 EXETER · DEVONSHIRE, LITTLE BRITAIN BAPTIST CHAPEL (1817).

153 LONDON · LYNDHURST ROAD CONGREGATIONAL CHURCH, HAMPSTEAD (1883–4).
A Victorian variant by Alfred Waterhouse on the Georgian octagonal plan.

154 WARMINGHURST · SUSSEX (13th-century church, 18th-century fittings). The plastered tympanum has a Royal coat of arms backed by painted curtains.

155 *left* MOLLAND · DEVONSHIRE (15th–16th-century church, 18th-century fittings). Other unrestored Devon churches are Buckerell, Cornworthy, Gittisham, Offwell, Parracombe, and West Ogwell.

STUART AND GEORGIAN CHURCHES

After the Fire of London in 1666 Sir Christopher Wren built and rebuilt a forest of churches in the square mile of the City under the dome of his new cathedral of St Paul's. He showed infinite ingenuity in his steeples of lead or stone and the buildings below them were of various shapes: some cruciform, some domed, some with aisles, some oblongs. All had prominent altars with carved altar pieces above them, rich pulpits and sounding boards, marble fonts with carved covers, high pews, and organ gallery. More were destroyed by the Victorians than by German bombing and most were unsympathetically adorned in the last half of the last century with stained glass. Wren's example was followed by his pupils in London and elsewhere. Many a squire who had built himself a fine new country house rebuilt the old parish church to match it. Expanding provincial towns at the end of the century had new churches built in them. The taste for Wren's style gave way to the flatter Roman manner of Chambers and the brothers Adam and in later Georgian times to the Greek Revival. Gothic of a romantic plaster-thin kind was revived in the eighteenth century. New shapes for churches were tried out such as circular or oval or rectangles with western portico and entrance instead of the usual north and south doors. But the compartmented plan still remained—a single altar in a chancel, however shallow, a nave and high pulpit, a font and baptistry pews, and if there was a gallery that is where the choir was. Village choirs were usually accompanied by their own instruments and town choirs had organs.

156 *right* CITY OF LONDON · ST VEDAST & ST MARY LE BOW. Steeples by Sir Christopher Wren—as seen before high buildings blotted them out.

158 NORTHAMPTON·NORTHAMPTONSHIRE, ALL SAINTS (1676–80). Built round the largely 14th-century tower after a fire in 1675, this interesting design is ascribed to Henry Bell of King's Lynn. The interior is a more homely provincial version of St Mary-at-Hill. The portico owes something to Inigo Jones's design for that of Old St Paul's, but is a very much humbler version, of 1701. In its centre is a weak statue of Charles the Second, 'Restoration rejoicing'.

159 INGESTRE·STAFFORDSHIRE (1673–6). A country church attributed to Sir Christopher Wren. It follows medieval plan and arrangement far more closely than many of his churches. Above engaged Tuscan columns with single abacus and circular arches rises a clerestory of round windows over a cornice. Ingestre is the most elaborate country church of its time.

157 *left* CITY OF LONDON·ST MARY-AT-HILL, LOVE LANE (1670–6). Into a roughly square space, Wren put a Greek cross, and over it a shallow coffered dome on pendentives borne by four broad arches springing from fluted columns. This City church retains its original atmosphere though altered in 1848 and furnished in Renaissance manner by William Gibbs-Rogers.

160 GAYHURST · BUCKINGHAMSHIRE (1728). A Georgian church in the grounds of an Elizabethan house. The architect of the church is unknown. The interior has all its Georgian fittings, a monument ascribed to Roubilliac, and windows of clear glass in rectangular panes.

161 GREENWICH · LONDON, ST ALPHEGE (1714–18). Eastern portico by Nicholas Hawksmoor.

162 CITY OF LONDON · ST MARY WOOLNOTH, LOMBARD STREET (1716–27). Hawksmoor's answer to the restrictions of a confined City site.

163 LONDON · ST GEORGE, BLOOMSBURY (1720–30).
By Nicholas Hawksmoor. He was careful to avoid
putting the steeple behind and above a portico
modelled on the Pantheon.

164 LONDON · ST MARTIN-IN-THE-FIELDS (1722–6).
By James Gibbs. He adopted the heavier, broader
proportions of the Roman Classical temple, adding
a steeple, placed astride the portico. The church set
a fashion. It was the most imitated of all Gibbs'
works, and he became the leader of early Georgian
Classical architects.

165 LONDON · ST MARY-LE-STRAND (1714–17). By James Gibbs. Now on an island in the middle of the Strand, it was originally surrounded by houses to the height of its first storey. The strong influence of Wren on James Gibbs is apparent in the semi-circular portico inspired by those to the transepts of St Paul's.

166 LONDON · ST MARY-LE-STRAND (1714–17).

167 WHITCHURCH (LITTLE STANMORE) · MIDDLESEX (1715). Built for the rich Duke of Chandos, of Canons, by John James. The interior of this ordinary church is decorated throughout with paintings and grisaille probably by Louis Laguerre and Antonio Bellucci, c 1720.

168 AYNHO · NORTHAMPTONSHIRE (1723). The influence of Vanbrugh is evident in the extremely domestic-looking side elevations to this Georgian church by Edward Wing, a local carpenter-architect. The medieval tower was retained.

169 SHOBDON · HEREFORDSHIRE (1753). The canopied pulpit has crimson velvet hangings with gold braid fringed tassels and embroidered 'glory'. The rococo Gothic interior combines something of the oriental *Chinoiserie* with the Walpole Strawberry Hill Gothick.

170 GREAT WITLEY · WORCESTERSHIRE (1735). A fully rococo church interior by an unknown architect under the influence of Gibbs. The gilt plasterwork and three paintings by Verrio were put in *c* 1747. The paintings, which adorn the ceiling, came with the ten windows of painted glass by Joshua Price from the Duke of Chandos' palace at Canons. The church was richly refurnished in *c* 1861. It is white and gold.

171 LANGTON-BY-SPILSBY · LINCOLNSHIRE (*c* 1750). A Georgian period interior with box pews of excellent workmanship arranged facing north and south as in a college chapel.

172 WANSTEAD · ESSEX (1787–90). An early work of Thomas Hardwick, Classical derived from Gibbs. The Gibbs influence died hard, even having a following of young men late in the century. Wanstead is a near-perfect interior, marred by Victorian stained glass. The pulpit is an unusual design. Beyond it is a monument by Van Nost to Sir Josiah Child (1699).

173 CITY OF LONDON · ALL HALLOWS, LONDON WALL (1765–7). By George Dance, Junior. A simple rectangular building with eastern apse. The coffered barrel ceiling rises from fluted attached Ionic columns without the usual cornice above the frieze. It is lit by lunette-shaped windows, an arrangement based on that of the Baths of Diocletian. This church is now used as a gallery by the Council for the Care of Churches.

174 GREAT PACKINGTON · WARWICKSHIRE (1790). By Joseph Bonomi, an Italian who worked for the Adam brothers, and later set up on his own. The plan is cross-shaped. It is red brick outside. Inside the walls are of smooth blocks of stone; the central space has a quadripartite vault. Light comes in through three semi-circular windows in the north, south, and west transepts.

175 GUNTON · NORFOLK (1769). Here the parish church is disguised as an Etruscan garden temple, the 18th-century landscapist's ideal, and set amidst ornamental shrubs in the grounds of the great house. The architect was Robert Adam, whose few other churches include Mistley, Essex, of which only the towers remain, and probably Binley, Warwickshire.

176 SHREWSBURY · SHROPSHIRE, ST CHAD (1790–2). This galleried rotunda was designed as an auditorium by George Steuart. The fine plaster ceiling in low delicate relief and the original woodwork suit this practical functional design.

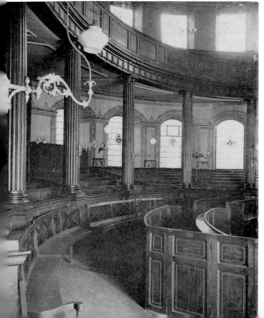

177 NEWCASTLE · NORTHUMBERLAND, ALL SAINTS (1786–96). By David Stephenson. An early example of the rotundas popular at the end of the 18th century and in the early years of the 19th. The architect, a local man, began as a carpenter; the woodwork is of mahogany.

178 TETBURY · GLOUCESTERSHIRE (1777–81). Designed and built by Francis Hiorn, this was the outstanding Gothic town church of the 18th century, and the internal arrangements escaped Victorian alterations until 1901. This photograph was taken before the east end was screened off and furnished as a chancel.

179 *below* THORPE MARKET · NORFOLK (1795). A delightful country version of the romantic early Gothic Revival.

180 *below right* THORPE MARKET · NORFOLK (1795). One of the thin Gothic windows filled with patterned leading and tinted coloured glass, set into the neat knapped flint walls.

MEMORIALS

After the Reformation people commemorated their families in stone and marble, instead of with prayers for the departed said at Mass. Chantry chapels became family pews with sculptured monuments on their walls. Most of our older churches contain handsome eighteenth-century sculpture. Headstones were put up in the churchyard outside to the lesser families. In districts where the stone or slate was available the churchyards are full of carved and engraved headstones often with touching epitaphs spaciously set out. The villa taste of modern parochial church councils has often caused these monuments of piety to be laid flat or stacked against the churchyard wall in order that the mower may more easily move among the Dorothy Perkins roses. Many country churchyards were disfigured before this with late Victorian tombs of Carrara marble from Italy and polished granite from Aberdeen and Cornwall.

181   OLD WOLVERTON · BUCKINGHAMSHIRE: THE MONUMENT TO SIR THOMAS LONGUEVILLE (1685). By an unknown sculptor.

182 SILTON · DORSET: PART OF MONUMENT TO SIR HUGH WYNDHAM (1684). By John Nost. The mourning figures lean away from the standing figure of the judge, tears streaming from their eyes.

183 STOKE DOYLE · NORTHAMPTONSHIRE: MONUMENT TO SIR EDWARD WARD (c 1720–5). This is an early work of J. M. Rysbrack, designed and carved soon after his arrival in England.

184　PUSEY · BERKSHIRE: MONUMENT TO JANE PUSEY (1724). Designed by a Flemish settler in England, Peter Scheemakers. Here the semi-reclining draped figure is backed by a reredos of veined marble into which is set a grey marble roundel recess with the bust of her husband.

185　SHERBORNE · GLOUCESTERSHIRE: MONUMENT TO JAMES DUTTON (1791). Signed and dated by the elder Richard Westmacott. The Angel of Life gazes mournfully on death. Under her left arm are draped portrait medallions of the deceased couple.

186 SWINBROOK · OXFORDSHIRE. During the 17th, 18th, and early 19th centuries the gravestone was the chief outlet for the expression of local masons and poets. Crudely carved cherubs with swags of foliage, or sometimes more ambitious decorative subjects, accompany epitaphs in country verse.

187 CHADDLEWORTH · BERKSHIRE (18th century).

188 SHILTON · OXFORDSHIRE. 18th-century headstones.

EARLY NINETEENTH-CENTURY CHURCHES

Steam power was changing England. The population suddenly increased, especially in the industrial north. There was not room in the old churches. Regency squares, terraces, and crescents appeared on the outskirts of the big towns; seaside watering places and inland spas grew. At the beginning of the century and in the century before, private chapels were built for distinguished preachers in the Church of England and called Proprietary chapels. In 1818 Parliament, alarmed at the spread of nonconformity and the possibility of the growth of atheism among the artisans as a result of the French Revolution, voted money for building churches of the Establishment and these were called Commissioners' Churches. Well-known architects were invited to design them and the style could be Classic or Gothic. If the former it was usually Greek, for interest in Athenian antiquities had supplanted interest in Rome. If Gothic was chosen the style was usually Perpendicular. The plan was always the same—an oblong with an altar at the east end, galleries round the three other sides, with an organ at the west and a western entrance with a tower so that the building would not look like a chapel. These Commissioners' Churches were built to house large congregations, usually as cheaply as possible.

189 TEIGNMOUTH · DEVONSHIRE, ST JAMES (1820). An octagonal preaching hall by Andrew Patey of Exeter, with cast-iron columns and plaster vaulting.

190 FLEET · DORSET (1827–9). Designed by a local man, Stickland.

191 LONDON · ST JOHN, DOWNSHIRE HILL, HAMP-
STEAD (1818). A rare surviving Evangelical estate
Proprietary chapel serving a district of neat stucco
houses. Proprietary chapels, common during the
early 19th century, were unendowed and un-
consecrated preaching houses built and owned by
trustees or proprietors to whom the congregation
paid rent for pews.

192 BUXTON · DERBYSHIRE, ST JOHN THE BAPTIST
(1811). Designed by Sir Jeffry Wyattville, this
church was built by the sixth Duke of Devonshire as the parish church of the new spa that his
father had begun.

193 LONDON · ALL SOULS, LANGHAM PLACE (1822–4). By John Nash, as part of his metropolitan improvements. The circular vestibule and its colonnaded spike disguised the change in direction between Nash's new Regent Street and the existing Portland Place. The outline has been ruined by the new B.B.C. extension since this photograph.

194 LONDON · ST ANNE, WANDSWORTH (1822–4). Sir Robert Smirke, designer of the British Museum, grafted Greek detail on to traditional Palladian plans. This resulted at Wandsworth in a giant Ionic portico and an attenuated cupola, each good in itself but odd together.

195 LONDON · ST MATTHEW, BRIXTON (1822). By C. F. Porden. Unlike Smirke's Wandsworth, this Greek Doric church, despite the English innovation of an eastern tower, is close to Grecian models. By placing the tower at the east end, C. F. Porden has avoided the mistake, which many of his contemporaries made, of combining a steeple with a western portico.

196 LONDON · ST JOHN, BETHNAL GREEN (1825–8). Here Sir John Soane has successfully solved an awkward problem of relating a tower to a façade engaged with it. The windows are evidence of the Victorian alterations within.

197 BRIGHTON · SUSSEX, ST PETER (1823–8). This early Gothic design, by Sir Charles Barry, the architect of the Houses of Parliament, lays emphasis on a west tower and portico; the church occupies a prominent site at the northern end of the Steyne.

198 *right* LONDON · ST LUKE, CHELSEA (1820–4). By James Savage, one of the first large town churches with consistent Gothic Revival detailing. The interior is vaulted in stone, but it has the feeling of plasterwork.

199 THEALE · BERKSHIRE (1820–32). In the design of this church, Edward Garbett, like Augustus Livesay at Andover, looked to Salisbury Cathedral, copying details and using them as a kit of parts with which to compose. The early 19th century saw the growth of research into medieval details.

200 CHELTENHAM · GLOUCESTERSHIRE, ST PETER (1840–9). By S. W. Dawkes, who could manage a wide repertoire of styles, this is in the Neo-Norman fashion of *c* 1840.

201 WILTON · WILTSHIRE (1841–5). This expensive Italianate masterpiece by two otherwise dull architects, Thomas Henry Wyatt and David Brandon, was dictated by the idiosyncratic taste of Princess Catharina Worontzov and her son Sidney, Lord Herbert of Lea. It is modelled on ancient Lombardic basilicas. Lord Herbert collected treasures from Italy and elsewhere for the interior.

VICTORIAN CHURCHES

This was the most prolific time of church building in English history. As the population was four times bigger than it was at the beginning of the century, it would have been surprising had this not been so. England was still Christian; there was now liberty of worship so that Roman Catholics, Methodists, Baptists, and many other denominations were building churches as fast as the Church of England. There are about 16,000 parishes in the Church of England and of these well over half have Victorian or later fabrics.

202 WICKHAM · BERKSHIRE (1845–9). By Benjamin Ferrey, Pugin's biographer. In the roof of the north aisle are painted and gilt *papier mâché* elephants brought from the 1863 Paris exhibition.

PUGIN AND THE MEDIEVALISTS

In 1841 A. W. N. Pugin, a witty and clever writer, draughtsman, and architect, and a convert to Rome, published his *Contrasts* at the age of twenty-nine. This and other books he published, until his death at the age of forty, put forward the theory that the only Christian architecture was Gothic; 1840 seemed to him inhuman and pagan. We must go back to 1440 to deep chancels, painted screens, twinkling lights, medieval-style glass, chasubles, orphreys, and incense. Pugin did the decoration and Gothic details of Barry's Houses of Parliament; he designed the medieval court in the Crystal Palace; he trained craftsmen to make church furniture and glass at Hardman's studio in Birmingham and himself built many churches. His ideas were taken up with great enthusiasm by the Church of England whose High Church movement was just then bringing the Gospel to industrial slums. If they could not have decent houses the workers should at least have uplifting churches. In old churches, box pews were replaced by open benches with free seats for all; galleries were cut down and choirs dressed in surplices were installed in chancels. Lights were put on altars and priests wore coloured stoles. Protestants or Evangelicals grew moustaches in revolt against the clean-shaven or bearded Tractarians—the High Church party. With the outward signs of revived Catholicism in the Church of England went deep piety and missionary vigour. It met with considerable opposition from the Protestant or Evangelical section of the Church which is why, to this day, box pews are more likely to be found in 'Low' churches than 'High' ones. There was also a moderate or Broad Church party between the two camps. The best known followers of Pugin who tried to build new churches which were copies of the old were Sir Gilbert Scott and R. C. Carpenter and Benjamin Ferrey.

203 RAMSGATE · KENT, ST AUGUSTINE (ROMAN CATHOLIC) (1847-52). Here Pugin was his own master, and here he fulfilled himself. The church glows with rich Hardman glass.

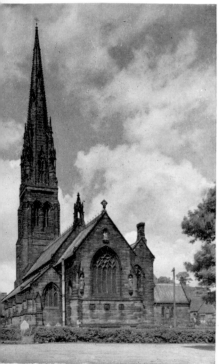

204 & 205 CHEADLE · STAFFORDSHIRE, ST GILES (ROMAN CATHOLIC) (1841-6). By Augustus Welby Northmore Pugin. The gilded rampant lions, the hinges of the west doors, show Pugin as an heraldic designer. Cheadle has painted and stencilled interior walls.

206 LONDON · ST MARY MAGDALENE, MUNSTER SQUARE (1849–52). By Richard Cromwell Carpenter (1812–1855). A Tractarian or High Church interior built on Pugin's principles of Gothic architecture.

207 *below right* HIGHNAM · GLOUCESTERSHIRE (1850). By Henry Woodyer for a rich and artistic client, Thomas Gambier Parry, the decorative artist.

208 LEAFIELD · OXFORD-SHIRE (1860). By Sir Gilbert Scott. Very few of the several hundreds of churches designed by Scott are original or interesting in themselves; seldom are their details free from mechanical copying. But they are all well built and substantial.

BEFORE AND AFTER
209 & 210

LONDON · ST ETHELBURGA, BISHOPSGATE. *left* Interior as shown in George Godwin Junior's *Churches of London 1839*. A modest late medieval interior with 1629 south gallery and three-decker pulpit, late 17th-century altar-piece, and box pews. The 15th-century tracery of stone has been removed from the windows and leaded clear lights substituted with panels of stained glass in the east window. The result is a characteristic adaptation of a small medieval church to prayer-book worship—a baptistry at the west end, a rich east end for the celebration of the other chief Sacrament, and pews and gallery in the nave arranged to be within sight of the reading desk for offices and the pulpit for exposition.

below The same interior 'restored' to the Victorian idea of a medieval church. All Classical woodwork, even that of 1629, has been removed. Perpendicular-style tracery and stained glass have been put back in the windows. The chancel is marked off from the nave by the stone cancellum with an iron screen above. The altar has been raised, the position of the pulpit changed, and the south aisle blocked with an organ. Since this last photograph was taken the church has been made more truly like its medieval self by the substitution of a wooden screen and loft, designed by Sir Ninian Comper, to replace the stone and iron.

Some church architects in the 1850s did not believe in copying old churches but in going on from where the Middle Ages left off. They used modern materials like brick and cast iron and gas lighting and coal heating. They planned churches in the Anglican manner with a prominent font and a prominent altar visible in its richly adorned chancel from all parts of the church. They did not hold with side altars. They also supervised the design of stained glass, hangings, and ironwork. One of them, George Edmund Street, the designer of the London Law Courts, was an artist who taught himself joinery and blacksmith's work as well as masonry and founded the Arts and Crafts movement of the Pre-Raphaelites and William Morris.

**211
&
212** LONDON · ALL SAINTS, MARGARET STREET (1850–9). By William Butterfield, the beginning of a new phase in the Gothic Revival. Here Butterfield used new industrial materials, a mauvish-red stock brick patterned with blue stock brick. He achieves a sense of space and height on a small cramped site. The interior effect of vastness and height is created by scale. There are strong contrasts of texture and colour.

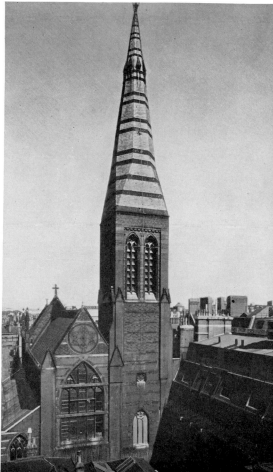

213 *above left* BABBACOMBE · DEVONSHIRE, ALL SAINTS (1868–74). By W. Butterfield. The bold use of shapes he invented himself, like this arch, and contrasting bricks, stones, and marbles, was copied by Butterfield's admirers.

214 *above right* GREENHAM · BERKSHIRE (1875–6, north aisle 1888). By Henry Woodyer (see 207) who was Butterfield's pupil. The capitals of this north aisle arcade were Woodyer's own invention, as are the roof and decoration of the chancel beyond.

215 *below left* LOWER SHUCKBURGH · WARWICKSHIRE (1864). By J. B. Crofts of Daventry, a local architect trying out originality with brick and stone.

216 LECKHAMPSTEAD · BERKSHIRE (1859). By Samuel Sanders Teulon. A Berkshire example of Victorian originality with use of brick in a brick and flint district.

217 & **218**

WESTCOTT · BUCKINGHAMSHIRE (1867). By G. E. Street. It was designed on Gothic principles without resort to unnecessary fripperies which were the bane of so many small Victorian churches built with limited funds. The plain austere interior (*below*) has uncarved capitals and pale brick walls.

219   FAWLEY · BERKSHIRE (1865–6). Breadth is a characteristic of many churches by Street. Street was a High Churchman, and the altar in most of his churches is prominent. Here it is backed by a reredos with a stone crucifixus against coloured tiles.

220   BRIGHTWALTON · BERKSHIRE (1862–3). By G. E. Street. Low columns in the nave were used to emphasize the height of the chancel. Interior walls are built of bare stone.

221   KINGSTON · DORSET (1874–80). By G. E. Street, and mostly built of local Purbeck by local labour from the quarries. Street said of this building, 'On the whole my jolliest church.'

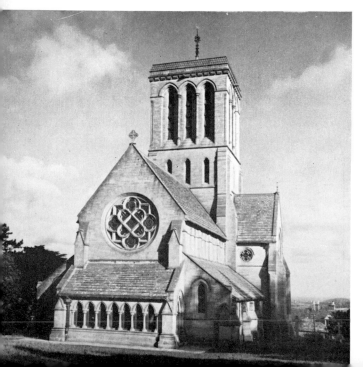

222 WALTHAM ABBEY · ESSEX (east window 1861). Occasionally some of the leading Pre-Raphaelite painters turned to designing stained glass. In this Burne-Jones excelled. He began in partnership with William Morris, and occasionally co-operated with Rossetti and Madox Brown. This Tree of Jesse window, designed in 1861, the central of his three east windows at Waltham Abbey, was executed by Powell. The east end of the Abbey was designed by William Burges.

223 BINGLEY · YORKSHIRE WEST RIDING, HOLY TRINITY (1866–8). One of the earliest works of Norman Shaw in partnership with W. Eden Nesfield; Shaw was chief draughtsman to Street before he set up on his own.

224 SKELTON · YORKSHIRE WEST RIDING (1871–2). By William Burges. This is the earlier of the two lavish churches in Yorkshire he designed. The later church is at Studley Royal. These two churches were built regardless of cost.

225 BRIGHTON · SUSSEX, ST MICHAEL. Nave designed by William Burges, 1863, but not built until 1893, twelve years after his death.

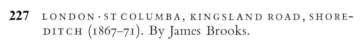

226 LONDON · ST CHAD, NICHOLS SQUARE, SHOREDITCH (1867–8). The several East London churches by the High-Church architect James Brooks are amongst the finest of the mid-Victorian period. They are in brick without fanciful details and decoration. St Chad is lofty with plate traceried windows over the windowless lean-to aisles of the nave, transepts, and stone vaulted apse.

227 LONDON · ST COLUMBA, KINGSLAND ROAD, SHORE-DITCH (1867–71). By James Brooks.

228 LONDON · ST LUKE, KENTISH TOWN (1868–70). By Basil Champneys, when a young man under the influence of Street and Burges.

229 BRIGHTON · SUSSEX, ST MARY (1877–9). By Sir William Emerson, a pupil of Burges. Emerson practised French Gothic in India, and later won the first competition for Liverpool Cathedral, but was passed over in the second for young Giles Gilbert Scott.

230 LONDON · ST PETER, VAUX-
HALL (1863–5). By J. L. Pearson.
It is a milestone in Pearson's
career, midway between his
early Pugin-type churches and
his own characteristic style.

231 LONDON · ST AUGUSTINE,
KILBURN (1870–80). J. L.
Pearson found his style late—
at the age of 53—in this
design, the greatest of London's
Victorian churches.

LATE VICTORIAN AND EDWARDIAN

There was now plenty of money for building new churches in the slums and middle-class
suburbs. Architects became interested less in style than in obtaining an internal effect of
height, lightness, and many vista'd splendour. Some, like George Gilbert Scott, Junior,
and G. F. Bodley, adapted Perpendicular; others like J. L. Pearson used Early English, and
some built with round-headed arches in simplified classical forms. The last Victorian, Sir
Ninian Comper, who died in 1960 aged 96 and started as a pupil of Bodley, was a daring
planner who introduced the first modern central altar, and his later churches could combine
Classic and Gothic motifs successfully in the same building.

232 CROYDON·SURREY, ST MICHAEL (1880–5). By J. L. Pearson. The Lady chapel.

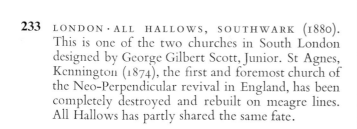

233 LONDON·ALL HALLOWS, SOUTHWARK (1880). This is one of the two churches in South London designed by George Gilbert Scott, Junior. St Agnes, Kennington (1874), the first and foremost church of the Neo-Perpendicular revival in England, has been completely destroyed and rebuilt on meagre lines. All Hallows has partly shared the same fate.

234 PENDLEBURY · LANCASHIRE, ST AUGUSTINE (1870–4). By G. F. Bodley. The buttresses supporting the roof of the nave have narrow arches for passage aisles cut through. Screen and reredos are by Bodley. The stained glass is by Kempe, with the deep greens and blues then coming into fashion.

Bedford Lemere

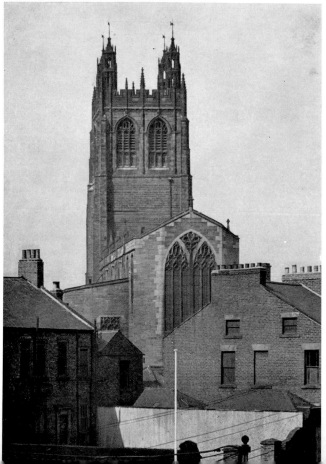

235 NEWCASTLE · NORTHUMBERLAND, ST MATTHEW (1877–1904). Designed by a local architect, R. J. Johnson, and completed by his pupils, Hicks and Charlewood.

236 LONDON · HOLY TRINITY, SLOANE STREET (1888–90). By J. D. Sedding, in an original Arts and Crafts free Perpendicular style that was later to become so popular. The furnishings and decorations in varied materials by varied artists are a pot-pourri of the best of the 1890s and make this church a permanent display of the work of the Arts and Crafts movement.

237 STOCKPORT · CHESHIRE, ST GEORGE (1893–7). By Paley and Austin.

Bedford Lemere

238 LONDON · THE HOLY REDEEMER, CLERKEN-WELL (1887–8). This Wren-Italianate interior, designed from the altar outwards, was Sedding's revolt against the conventional Gothic of the 1880s, which was in danger of growing stale. Outside, an Italianate campanile designed by Sedding's pupil, Harry Wilson, fronts the busy Exmouth Market full of Cockney voices and Italian faces.

239 LONDON · BROMPTON ORATORY (ROMAN CATHOLIC) (1878, work begun 1880, completed 1884, the dome 1896). A competition for the London Oratory in 1878 was won by Herbert Gribble, whose Italian Renaissance design fully satisfied the Italian tastes of the founders, Cardinal Newman and Father Faber. The church is the victory of a school of Roman Catholic taste, in which Father Faber was prominent, that looked to modern Rome for inspiration, and opposed Pugin's Gothic aestheticism. The rich decorations of the nave by C. T. G. Formilli help create the effect of Italian Baroque splendour which the northern light makes dark despite the innovation of skylight domes.

240 BRIGHTON · SUSSEX, ST BARTHOLOMEW. This marble pulpit (1906) is one of several furnishings by Harry Wilson in this outsize Noah's Ark in brick (built 1874), the masterpiece of a local architect, Edmund Scott. With a height of 135 feet from pavement to roof ridge, it is the tallest parish church in Britain.

241 KEMPLEY · GLOUCESTERSHIRE, NEW CHURCH (1903). By A. Randall Wells. The Arts and Crafts revolt against the last phase of the Gothic Revival. Randall Wells designed one other church, St Wilfrid, Halton, Leeds (1937–9).

242 CHARTERHOUSE-ON-MENDIP · SOMERSET (1908). Designed by W. D. Caröe, architect to the Ecclesiastical Commissioners, a protagonist of *Art Nouveau* Gothic.

243 MALVERN LINK·WORCESTER-
SHIRE, THE ASCENSION (1903).
By Sir Walter Tapper.

244 LONDON · THE ANNUNCIATION,
BRYANSTON STREET (1913–14). By
Sir Walter Tapper.

245 LONDON · ALL SAINTS, TOOTING GRAVENEY (1905–6). Designed by Temple Moore, most of whose work was done in Yorkshire. The Baroque reredos came from Bologna; the pulpit was designed by Sir Walter Tapper.

246 BITTERNE PARK · SOUTHAMPTON, HAMPSHIRE, THE ASCENSION (1924–6). By Sir Charles Nicholson. Of all the church architects of the early 20th century, Nicholson was the most prolific. After work more influenced by his early partner, Micklethwaite, and by Bodley, than by his master, J. D. Sedding, Nicholson turned towards a wide variety of styles. The church has a series of stained-glass windows by the architect's brother, A. K. Nicholson, and G. E. R. Smith. The Renaissance screen is the last work of Randoll Blacking.

247 SOUTHEND · KENT, ST JOHN (1928). Designed by Sir Charles Nicholson.

248 HAMPDEN PARK · EASTBOURNE, SUSSEX, ST MARY (1955). By Sir Edward Maufe, architect of Guildford Cathedral. A small and friendly church for a mid-wars building estate. Choir and sanctuary are seen from the nave. Sir Edward uses a simplified Gothic recalling the work of Temple Moore. He is interested in furniture design, fabrics, and stained glass in the old Arts and Crafts tradition, so that the interiors of his churches all hang together. Influenced by Swedish art, he generally uses pastel shades.

249 TERRIERS · HIGH WYCOMBE, BUCKINGHAMSHIRE (1930). By Sir Giles Gilbert Scott, architect of Liverpool Cathedral. Like his grandfather, Sir Gilbert Scott, he often liked to divide nave from chancel by a central tower whose lower windows admitted light and so caused an internal effect of rays of daylight from a hidden source dividing the nave from a darker chancel beyond. He also was skilled in the use of local stone and here has employed Buckinghamshire flints with lime-stone dressings for a church in his own individual style of Gothic.

250 WELLINGBOROUGH · NORTHAMPTONSHIRE, ST MARY (begun 1906, structurally complete 1932). In this church, generally considered to be his masterpiece, Sir Ninian Comper has blended Classic and Gothic in one, in what he called 'unity by inclusion'; that is to say he blended Classic and Gothic motives as in these brown ironstone columns with their Greek Doric fluting supporting a Gothic roof.

251 CARSHALTON · SURREY. This blue-and-gold organ gallery and case (1931–c 1941) are part of Sir Ninian Comper's re-decoration of a church rebuilt by the Blomfields.

252 COSHAM · HAMPSHIRE, ST PHILIP (1938). By Sir Ninian Comper. The high altar under its gold ciborium has room for communicants round all four sides, the altar beyond it being that of the Lady chapel. Classic columns support Gothic vaulting and the capitals are Comper's invention.

253 BOURNEMOUTH · HAMPSHIRE, ST FRANCIS (1929). This white-walled Italianate church by J. Harold Gibbons looks like the church of some Anglo-Catholic mission in South Africa.

254 *below left* LONDON · ST ANSELM, KENNINGTON (1933). By Adshead and Ramsey. The bare white-walled interior of this vaguely Byzantine-style church is Early Christian in feeling, though the excellent furnishings are arranged in the characteristic 19th-century Tractarian Anglican way, the choir stalls being placed between the altar and the benches of the congregation.

255 *below right* LONDON · ST SAVIOUR, ELTHAM (1933). By Cachemaille-Day, Welch, and Lander, and one of the most talked-of church interiors of the 1930s. This austere church has not dated so badly as most others in the highly streamlined vogue of the 1930s.

MODERN

At the beginning of the pictures in this book is one of the stone crosses set up over a thousand years ago to show that a district, which was once an inhabited forest clearing or a village on a hill top, had received Christianity. Today on the big new housing estates, it is only possible to distinguish a church from a public library, school, or small factory by a cross on its wall or above it, and even then it is not easy to know to what denomination it belongs. New churches today have to be provided with a social hall, a canteen, offices, and lavatories as well as the place of worship itself where are font and altar. Churches start, as they always do when on a mission, with the priest going to live among the people and holding his first services in a house or temporary hut. This is one of the reasons why, compared with Edwardian splendour, the buildings that follow look rather bare. Another reason is fashion and a third is that architecture today is more a matter of assembling factory-made prefabricated parts in agreeable and practicable shapes than of handicraft. The artist has his chance in painting on walls, making stained glass, and carving figures.

256 *below left* LONDON · THE DANISH SEAMEN'S CHURCH, COMMERCIAL ROAD, STEPNEY (1956–9). By the Danish architect Holger Jensen of Copenhagen, in association with Edward Armstrong and Frederick McManus, this church forms a group with a social centre for Danish seamen. There is little difference between modern churches in England and those in any other country. This is not an English church, but it illustrates the international style.

257 *below right* SHEFFIELD · YORKSHIRE WEST RIDING, ST CATHERINE, WOODTHORPE (1960–1). By Sir Basil Spence. The altar is set in a shallow apse.

258 LONDON · ST PAUL, BOW COMMON, STEPNEY (1958–60). Designed by Robert Maguire and Keith Murray.

259 LONDON · ST PAUL, BOW COMMON, STEPNEY (1958–60). The interior is an aisled, square brick hall, lit from above by a Rhenish helm-crowned glass lantern. The free-standing altar beneath its ciborium stands towards the centre of the church, as in Comper's church of St Philip, Cosham. (See **252**.)

260 LONDON · CONGREGATIONAL CHURCH, BLACKHEATH (1958). Designed by Trevor Danatt. Big curtains of glass hang between ragstone buttresses.

261 MITCHAM GREEN · SURREY, METHODIST CHURCH (1958). Designed by Edward D. Mills. The wall of rough cut slabs of York stone forms a textured background to the small Communion table.

262 KETTLEWELL · YORKSHIRE WEST RIDING, SCARGILL HOUSE CHAPEL (1961–2). By George Pace. A chapel of a Church of England holiday and conference centre, placed on a hillside and backed by woods. The steeply pitched roof sweeps up from low, lean-to aisles, whose low stone walls seem to grow out of the hillside.

263 FARNHAM ROYAL · BUCKINGHAMSHIRE, ST GEORGE (1960–1). By Henry Braddock and D. F. Martin-Smith. The fan-shaped plan of this building radiates from the altar which is placed beneath a curtain of stained glass, by John Baker, set in concrete. After the dramatic, towering figures of the Madonna and Child in a raised east end, the thin campanile seems starved.

Acknowledgement to photographers

Architect and Building News 254
Hallam Ashley 150

M. W. Barley 51, 171
G. L. Barnes 226, 227, 233, 245, 247
Bedford Lemere 234, 237
G. H. Birch: *London Churches of the XVIIth and XVIIIth centuries* 156, 157
Bitterne Studios 246

N. F. Cachmaille-Day 255
Gerald Cobb 64, 178
Kenneth Cole 72
Council for the Care of Churches 27, 29, 35, 61, 107, 115, 121, 215, 253
Country Life 16, 139
Crown copyright, reproduced by permission of the Controller of H.M. Stationery Office 32, 36, 71, 103, 123, 125, 135, 137, 140, 144, 190
Mrs Crossley 10, 11, 34, 40, 50, 60, 66, 75, 86, 106, 109, 111, 118, 120, 128, 132, 155

Trevor Dannatt 260

Helmut Gernsheim 28
George Godwin, jun: *Churches of London 1839* 209
Norman Gold Photography 258, 259
Cecil H. Greville 263

Leo Herbert-Felton 162
Mrs Yvonne Howard 9
Rodney Hubbuck 20, 69, 70

A. F. Kersting 152, 161, 163, 164, 166, 173, 193, 196, 198, 222

E. C. LeGrice 49
Quentin Lloyd 124, 143
E. Lovell, Ipswich 99

John McCann 148, 256
G. B. Mason 159
Sir Edward Maufe 248
Eric Meadows 17, 84
Mrs G. Munday 136

Mrs Doris Nelson 170
Sydney Newbery 251

George G. Pace 262
John Piper 1, 6, 12, 22, 23, 24, 31, 39, 42, 48, 52, 55, 56, 58, 62, 76, 78, 79, 91, 95, 96, 97, 98, 110, 112, 114, 129, 133, 145, 146, 179, 180, 181, 182, 184, 186, 187, 188, 192, 199, 202, 208, 214, 216, 217, 218, 219, 220, 224

Sir Giles Scott 249
Henk Snoek 257, 261
P. S. Spokes 169
Studio Blake 252
Studio Vista Limited 153

M. Tapper 243, 244
Mrs Tomlinson 127

Charles White, Press and Commercial Photographer 59
F. R. Winstone 151
Wisbech Museum 53

INDEX TO TEXT

Adam, Robert 39
Alne, Yorks 23
America, churches in 36
Anne, Queen 35
Archer, Thomas 36
Attempt to Discriminate the Styles of English Architecture 13
Augustine, St 7, 8

Bassa, priest 8
Bedfordshire churches 26
Bentley, J. F. 49
Berkshire churches 35
Bertha, Queen 8
Bidlake, W. H. 48
Birmingham, St Philip 36
Biscop, Benedict 8
Black Death 21, 22
Blomfield, Sir A. W. 47
Bloomsbury, St George 35
Bodley, G. F. 47, 51
Book of Common Prayer, 1549 26
 1662 33
Boston, Lincs 20
Bournemouth, Hants, churches in 52
Bradwell-on-Sea, Essex 8
Brighton, Sussex, churches in 52
Bristol, churches in 52
 Highbury Chapel 49
Brixworth, Northants 8
Burton-on-Trent, Staffs 28
Butterfield, W. 46, 49

Canterbury, Kent, Cathedral 22
 St Pancras 7
 SS Peter and Paul 7
Caroë, W. D. 52
Carpenter, R. C. 45
Catterick, Yorks 27
Chapel and School Architecture 49–50
Charles I, King 32
 II, King 33, 34
Chatwin, J. A. 48
Cheadle, Staffs, St Giles 49
Chellaston, Derby. 28
Cheshire churches 26
Church Building Society 40, 44
Churches, Mission Halls and Schools 50
Cobbett, W. 19
Commissioners' Churches 40
Comper, Sir J. N. 53, 55
Cornwall churches 25, 29
Crakehall, Richard of 27
Crouch and Butler 50

Decorated style 18–20
Denys, Roger 27
Deptford, St Paul 36
Derby, All Saints 36
Devon churches 25, 29
Dickinson, W. 35
Dorset churches 25
Douglas, J. 48
Dunstan, St 9

Early English style 15–18
Eastbourne, churches in 52
Ecclesiological Society 46
Ecclesiology 42–43
Edward II, King 22
 VI, King 31
Eighteenth-century churches 35–39
Elizabeth I, Queen 31
Escomb, Durham 9
Esher, Surrey 43
Ethelbert, King 7, 8

Ferguson, C. J. 48
Fifty New Churches 35–36

Finsbury, Wesley's Chapel 39, 50
Fishlake, Yorks 24
Fotheringhay, Northants 27
Fowler, C. H. 48
  J. 48
French Gothic 46

George I, King 35
Gerrards Cross, Bucks 48
Gibbs, J. 35, 36
Gloucester, Cathedral 22
Gloucestershire churches 25
Goldie, G. 49
Goodhart-Rendel, H. S. 48
Gothic, Meaning of word 15
  Revival of 38–39, 40–48
  Rise of 12–13
Gray, Rev. W. 26
Great Paxton, Hunts 9
Greenwich, St Alphege 35
Groombridge, Kent 32

Hadfield, M. E. 49
Hampshire churches 25
Hansom, J. A. 49
Harvey, J. 27
Hawksmoor, N. 35
Henry VIII, King 31
Hertfordshire churches 26
Hexham, Northumb 9
Hiorne, F. 39
Holborn, St Alban 46
Horwood, W. 27
Huntingdonshire churches 26

India, churches in 36
Ipswich, Suff., Unitarian Chapel 34

James, J. 35
Jarrow, Dur. 8–9
Jobson, F. J. 49
Jones, Inigo 32

Keeling, E. Bassett 48
Kennington, St Agnes 48
Kent churches 25
Kirk, C. 48

Lamb, E. B. 48
Lancashire churches 26
Langton by Spilsby, Lincs 38
Laud, Archbishop W. 32

Leeds, St John 32
Leighton Bromswold, Hunts 32–33
Limehouse, St Anne 35
Lincolnshire churches 15, 26
London, New St Paul's 33, 35
  Old St Paul's 22, 33
  St Benet Fink 33
  St Catherine Cree 33
  St Mary Woolnoth 35
Louth, Lincs 26
Lydd, Kent 9

Mary, Queen 31
Minstead, Hants 43
Monkwearmouth, Dur. 8, 24
Moore, T. L. 51
Morris, W. 45

Nineteenth-century churches 40–48
Nonconformist churches, 18th-century 39
  19th-century 49–50
  20th-century 53–54
Norfolk churches 15, 26, 31
Norman churches 10–12
Northamptonshire churches 26
Norwich, Old Meeting 34
Nottingham 28

Palladio, Andrea 36
Paulinus of Nola 7
Pearson, J. L. 47
Perpendicular style 22–26
Plaxtol, Kent 33
Porticus 7–8
Prynne, G. H. F. 52
Pugin, A. W. N. 41–43, 48–49, 50
  E. W. 49
Puritan party 31

Quebec, Cathedral 36

Ramsgate, St Augustine 42, 49
Reculver, Kent 8
Renaissance 32
Restoration of churches 43–45
Rickman, Thomas 13, 14, 18, 23, 40
Ripon, Yorks 9
Roman Catholic churches, 18th-century 39
  19th-century 48–49
  20th-century 54
Romanesque 7–12

St Leonards, churches in 52
St Marylebone, All Saints, Margaret Street 46
  St Peter, Vere Street 36
Saxon churches 9–12
Scotland, Presbyterian churches 34
Scott, Sir G. G. 16, 47–48
  G. G. 48, 50
  J. O. 48
Shrewsbury, Earl of 49
Smith, F. 36
Somerset churches 25
Southwark, All Hallows 48
Spitalfields, Christchurch 35
Staunton Harold, Leics 33
Stepney, St George in the East 35
Stoke Newington, St Matthias 46
Street, G. E. 27, 46–47
Suburbs, churches in 51–52
Suffolk churches 26
Surrey churches 25
Sussex churches 15, 25

Taylor, M. and H. 48
Tetbury, Glos 39
Tite, Sir W. 48
Transitional style 14
True Principles of Gothic 41–43
Twentieth-century churches 51–54

Vanbrugh, Sir J. 35
Walpole St Peter, Norf. 20
Wardell, W. W. 49
Waterloo Churches 40
Watford, Herts, Holy Rood 49
Waverley Abbey, Surrey 11
Westminster, Banqueting Hall, Whitehall 32
  Queen's Chapel 32
  Royal Chapel 22
  St George, Hanover Square 36
  St James, Piccadilly 34, 36
  St John 36
  St Martin-in-the-Fields 36, 37
  St Mary le Strand 36
Wesley, John 39
Whitby, Synod of 7, 8
William III, King 34
Wiltshire churches 25
Windsor, Berks 22
Wing, Bucks 9, 10
Worth, Sussex 9–10
Wren, Sir C. 17, 33–34, 35
Wulfstan, Bishop 10
Wyatt, J. 39
Wyberton, Lincs 27
Wykenham, William of 26

York 28
Yorkshire churches 26

INDEX TO ILLUSTRATIONS

The numbers refer to the illustrations

Abbey Dore, Here. 32
Abbotsbury, Dorset 144
Ampney St Mary, Glos 122
Ashbourne, Derby. 34
Astbury, Ches. 66
Aynho, Northants 168

Babbacombe, Devon. 213
Barton-on-Humber, Lincs 8
Barton-under-Needwood, Staffs 126
Batcombe, Som. 78
Beaminster, Dorset 71
Beetham, Westmor. 118
Beverley, Yorks, Minster 47
St Mary 86, 87
Bighton, Hants 27
Bingley, Yorks 223
Birkin, Yorks 19
Bitterne Park, Hants 246
Bledington, Glos 83
Blisland, Corn. 64
Blythburgh, Suff. 97
Bottesford, Lincs 41
Bournemouth, Hants 253
Boxgrove, Sussex 30, 127
Bradwell-juxta-Coggeshall, Essex 140
Bridlington, Yorks 43, 85
Brighton, Sussex, St Bartholomew 240
St Mary 229
St Michael 225
St Peter 197
Brightwalton, Berks 220
Bristol, St Mary, Redcliffe 65
Wesley's Chapel 151
Brougham, Westmor. 137
Burwell, Cambs 88
Buxton, Derby. 192

Carshalton, Surrey 251
Chaddleworth, Berks 187
Charterhouse-on-Mendip, Som. 242
Cheadle, Staffs 204, 205
Cheltenham, Glos 200
Christchurch, Hants 29, 61
Church Hanborough, Oxon 111
Cirencester, Glos 81, 104
Clayton, Sussex 28
Coln Rogers, Glos 119
Combe, Oxon 117
Cosham, Hants 252
Coventry, War. 101
Crewkerne, Som. 73
Croscombe, Som. 132
Croydon, Surrey 232

Dartmouth, Devon. 106
Dennington, Suff. 110
Denston, Suff. 99
Dorchester, Oxon 55
Dunstable, Beds 17

East Hendred, Berks 39
Eaton Bray, Beds 44
Edington, Wilts. 60
Elkstone, Glos 25
Escomb, Dur. 3, 4
Ewelme, Oxon 109
Exeter, Devon. 152
Eye, Suff. 98

Fairfield, Kent 143
Farnham Royal, Bucks 263
Fawley, Berks 219
Fingest, Bucks 12
Fishlake, Yorks 23, 24
Fleet, Dorset 190
Fleet, Lincs 52
Framlingham, Suff. 96, 133

Gatcombe, I.o.W. 72
Gayhurst, Bucks 160
Glastonbury, Som. 77
Great Packington, War. 174
Great Witley, Worcs 170
Greenham, Bucks 214
Gunton, Norf. 175
Guyhirn, Cambs 136

Hampden Park, Sussex 248
Hamstall Ridware, Staffs 63
Hanwell, Oxon 56
Hawton, Notts 57
Headbourne Worthy, Hants 5
Hessett, Suff. 114
Higham Ferrers, Northants 54
Highnam, Glos 207
Holcombe, Som. 141
Howden, Yorks 45

Ingestre, Staffs 159
Ipplepen, Devon. 75
Isle Abbots, Som. 76

Kempley, Glos, New Church 241
    Old Church 26
Kettlewell, Yorks 262
Kilpeck, Here. 20
Kinlet, Salop 112
King's Lynn, Norf. 91
Kingston, Dorset 221
Kirkby Lonsdale, Westmor. 11
Kirkstead, Lincs 38

Langley, Salop 130
Langridge, Som. 22
Langton-by-Spilsby, Lincs 171
Lastingham, Yorks 10
Launceston, Corn. 68
Leafield, Oxon 208
Leckhampstead, Berks 216
Ledbury, Here. 49
Leeds, Yorks 131
London, All Hallows, London Wall 173
    All Hallows, Southwark 233
    All Saints, Margaret Street 211, 212
    All Saints, Tooting Graveney 245
    All Souls, Langham Place 193
    Annunciation, Bryanston Street 244
    Blackheath Congregational church 260
    Brompton Oratory 239

Danish Seamen's church, Commercial Road
    256
Holy Redeemer, Clerkenwell 238
Holy Trinity, Sloane Street 236
Lyndhurst Road Congregational church,
    Hampstead 153
St Alphege, Greenwich 161
St Anne, Wandsworth 194
St Anselm, Kennington 254
St Augustine, Kilburn 231
St Chad, Shoreditch 226
St Columba, Shoreditch 227
St Ethelburga, Bishopsgate Street 209, 210
St George, Bloomsbury 163
St John, Bethnal Green 196
St John, Downshire Hill, Hampstead 191
St Luke, Chelsea 198
St Luke, Kentish Town 228
St Martin-in-the-Fields, Westminster 164
St Mary-at-Hill, Love Lane 157
St Mary Le Bow, Cheapside 156
St Mary-le-Strand, Westminster 165, 166
St Mary Magdalene, Munster Square 206
St Mary Woolnoth, Lombard Street 162
St Matthew, Brixton 195
St Paul, Bow Common 258, 259
St Peter, Vauxhall 230
St Saviour, Eltham 255
St Vedast, Foster Lane 156
Long Sutton, Lincs 42
Lower Shuckburgh, War. 215
Luton, Beds 84

Madley, Here. 36
Malpas, Ches. 67
Malvern Link, Worcs 243
Melbourne, Derby. 14
Minster-in-Thanet, Kent 37
Mitcham Green, Surrey 261
Molland, Devon. 155
Munslow, Salop 48

Navenby, Lincs 51
Newcastle, Northumb., All Saints 177
    St Matthew 235
Norbury, Derby. 50
Northampton 158
Norwich, Norf. 150

Oddington, Glos. 33
Old Wolverton, Bucks 181

Othery, Som. 116
Oxford 135

Patrington, Yorks 46
Pendlebury, Lancs 234
Penhurst, Sussex 124
Pershore, Worcs 35
Pillerton Hersey, War. 40
Porchester, Hants 16
Puddletown, Dorset 139
Pusey, Berks 184

Quenington, Glos 13

Raddington, Som. 121
Ramsgate, Kent 203
Ranworth, Norf. 108
Repton, Derby. 2
Romsey, Hants 18
Ruishton, Som. 79

St Blazey, Corn. 69
St Osyth, Essex 125
Salle, Norf. 90
Sefton, Lancs 128
Selham, Sussex 7
Sheffield, Yorks 257
Shelton, Norf. 92
Sherborne, Dorset 103
Sherborne, Glos 185
Shilton, Oxon 188
Shobdon, Here. 169
Shottesbrooke, Berks 62
Shrewsbury, Salop 176
Silton, Dorset 182
Skelton, Yorks 224
South Creake, Norf. 93
Southend, Kent 247
Steeple Ashton, Wilts. 80
Steetley, Derby. 21
Stock, Essex 123
Stockport, Ches. 237
Stoke-by-Nayland, Suff. 94, 105
Stoke Doyle, Northants 183

Stonegrave, Yorks 1
Strensham, Worcs 134
Sunningwell, Berks 129
Swinbrook, Oxon 186
Syleham, Suff. 95

Talland, Corn. 107
Teignmouth, Devon. 189
Terriers, Bucks 249
Tetbury, Glos 178
Tewkesbury, Glos 15, 115
Thaxted, Essex 100
Theale, Berks 199
Thorpe Market, Norf. 179, 180
Thorpe-next-Haddiscoe, Norf. 9
Trotton, Sussex 59
Tydd St Mary, Lincs 53

Uffington, Berks 31

Walpole, Suff. 149
Walpole St Peter, Norf. 89
Waltham Abbey, Essex 222
Wanstead, Essex 172
Warham St Mary, Norf. 147
Warminghurst, Sussex 154
Warwick 102, 113
Wasing, Berks 145
Wellingborough, Northants 250
Westcott, Bucks 217, 218
Whitby, Yorks 138
Whitchurch, Middx. 167
Wickham, Berks 202
Widford, Oxon 146
Wilton, Wilts. 201
Winchcombe, Glos 82
Winslow, Bucks 148
Winterbourne St Martin, Dorset 70
Winterbourne Tomson, Dorset 142
Wolfhamcote, War. 58
Wormington, Glos 6
Wrington, Som. 74

Yarnton, Oxon 120